Building a Successful High School Sports Program

DeAngelo Wiser

DARK
RIVER

An imprint of Bennion Kearny Ltd.

To Mom and Dad, Christine and Jimmie. The lessons and challenges we faced together shaped my determination. No one sacrificed more for their children. To my sister and brother-in-law, DeAnna and Aubrey. Your guidance and influence was always a shining light. So thankful.

Acknowledgements

I want to thank all those who contributed to this book. Bill Beswick, Molly Grishman, Dave Barney, Jody Hamilton, Jean Kesterson, Aaron Ocampo, Mike Bowlin, Karen Vanover, Cy Tucker, Bob Koski, Daniel Sandlin, and Kevin Wright. These coaches, leadership consultants and athletic directors, who have combined for more than 90 team and individual state championships, continue to set the standard for all coaches and administrators to emulate. Through their willingness to share their experience and insight we are all better prepared to positively impact our players. Thank you all so much.

My wife has always supported my efforts to give something back to the coaching community and provide leadership to all teams. My work is a reflection of her encouragement and drive to never give up and keep pursuing your dreams. I am truly blessed to be a part of her life.

Many thanks to James Lumsden-Cook who worked tirelessly on every aspect of putting this work together for Bennion Kearny. Without his guidance and expertise, we would not be able to share this work with all the coaches.

To all my former and current players, coaches, officials and colleagues, this work is a joyous passion that allows me to relive some beautiful memories and challenges that we all worked together to solve. I truly believe they made us better people, and I am so grateful the game brought us together. I will never forget you. God Bless You.

Keep Inspiring!

Testimonials

"In a very elite class of coaches"
I have worked with hundreds of coaches over the years, and there is no doubt that Coach DeAngelo Wiser is in a very elite class of coaches who understand the true value of sport. Coach Wiser's teams are not only well-coached in the sport of soccer, but his athletes are also highly motivated. Using a people-building methodology, Coach Wiser teaches his teams all of the important values inherent in sport – teamwork, character, discipline, and positivity – just to name a few.
Jason Neidell
Head Coach, Western Kentucky University Women's Soccer

"The legacy you leave"
I've been involved in athletics for 27 years and have never been around someone that truly understood athletics and life in a way that Coach Wiser has shown me. One of the greatest gifts as a coach is to know that your players leave your program better people. Getting the chance as an athletic director to work with him, and getting to know him on a personal level, he has changed the way I look at life and how I approach athletics. One of my favorite quotes is "Let someone else praise you and not your own mouth, a stranger, and not your own lips." Coach Wiser is one of the most humble coaches and would go out of his way to make sure you received recognition over him. He is one of a kind and in my eyes he is our John Wooden.
Daniel Sandlin
Former Athletic Director
East Jessamine High & Middle Schools

"The right decision"
I was blessed to work with Coach Wiser for seven years in a classroom setting. He always had a plan and could see the big picture at all times. His coaching wisdom, ability to motivate people, calm demeanor, and thoughtfulness were displayed every day. His common message was the right decision is not always easy and the easy decision is not always right. I am a much better coach, person and teacher for having spent part of my career with him. I am forever grateful for our time together.
Mike Bowlin
Head Football Coach
East Jessamine High School

"Leader and Role Model"

As superintendent of Jessamine County Schools for nine years, I had the privilege of working with hundreds of coaches – most of whom were exceptional men and women who loved their athletes and their sport. DeAngelo Wiser stands out among that elite group as a leader and a standard-bearer. The words that come to mind when I think of Coach Wiser are humble, kind, and devoted. He is a man of character known for his integrity and commitment to his athletes above self and status. He was a celebrated coach, but, more importantly, he was a role model for his players, their families, and his colleagues.

Lu Young
University of Kentucky College of Education Faculty Member
Former Superintendent
Jessamine County Schools

"A classroom on grass"

Coach Wiser's commitment and passion for his players to excel not only on the field but also in the classroom was evident from my first conversation with him. Coach Wiser is truly a "players' coach." His knowledge of the game and manner in which he coaches is truly a classroom on grass. There is constant reinforcement and enthusiasm challenging each player to improve daily. DeAngelo Wiser is a role model for those who aspire to be a head coach in any sport.

Ken Cox
Former District Athletic Director
Jessamine County Schools

About this Book's Contributors

Beswick, Bill. A leading applied performance psychologist who specializes in working with elite teams. In soccer, Bill has worked at Manchester United, Derby County, Middlesbrough, and Sunderland in the English Premier League and with FC Twente in the Dutch Eredivisie, where he supported Women's and Academy teams as well as the first team. He has contributed to Pro Licence award courses for a number of European Football Associations and has international experience with the England U18 and U21 squads and as Team Psychologist with England Senior Men. This season, 2017/18, he is working with Bristol City FC in the English Championship League. He specializes in 'coaching the coach' and is mentoring soccer coaches at National Team and Club levels across the globe.

His first book 'Focused For Soccer' published by Human Kinetics and in a new, enlarged 2nd edition, was one of the first to explore the psychology of football and has proved to be a sustained success, with translations into seven languages including Japanese, Chinese, Spanish and German. In 2015 'One Goal – The Mindset of Winning Soccer Teams' was published. Via his website www.billbeswick.com, Bill's expanding range of themed sports psychology topics provide coaches and players with unique performance development resources presented in accessible, downloadable formats and based on more than 40 years of coaching and teaching experience.

As well as working with elite teams and coaches across many different sports, Bill's career has included coaching under-8 mini rugby, school team sports, and men's and women's student and representative basketball teams. The importance of participation, enjoyment, and involvement in sport at whatever level has always been part of his life. Ask Bill what his most fulfilling role is and he'll reply "Coaching Coaches". It is as a coach educator and mentor that his experience and insights prove the most valuable.

Barney, Dave. Dave has coached varsity athletics at Albuquerque Academy for 50 years, and boys and girls swimming for the past 42 years. His swim teams have won 38 New Mexico high school state championships. He has been inducted into 6 Halls of Fame, including the University of New Mexico's Athletic Hall of Honor, the National Federation of High School Athletics Hall of Fame, the State of New Mexico's Sports Hall of Fame, and the National Interscholastic Swim Coaches Hall of Fame. In 2006, he became one of the first coaches named as a David H. Robertson National Honor Coach. In March of 2018, he will receive NISCA's most prestigious award, the Collegiate-Scholastic Coaches Award. He is currently a member of the International Hall of Fame's nominating and selection committee. Locally, he is perhaps better known as the founder of the Sundance Aquatic Association, the state's largest single swimming body for the last 45 years. He serves the profession of architecture as an aquatic design consultant for several architectural firms. In that regard, the most precious of his designs was his part in the aquatic design of the Academy's nationally regarded natatorium. He is a writer and frequent lecturer on all matters pertaining to sports history. He grew up in various parts of the world competing in football, ice hockey, and baseball. In college, he was a three-sport athlete. Never, during that time, did he ever give any thought to becoming a swim coach. *Chapters 10, 18, and 20*

Bowlin, Mike. Head Football Coach at East Jessamine High School. Four-time Ohio Valley Conference Champion as a player at Eastern Kentucky University. District Coach of the Year, 2006, 2010, 2014, 2016. Kentucky/Tennessee All-Star Game Coach 2015. Winningest football coach in East Jessamine history. *Chapter 27*

Grisham, Molly. Owner, Influencer, and Lead Facilitator at Influence LLC. Molly is passionate about personal growth, leadership development, communication, problem-solving, service learning, and conflict resolution. A visionary with a heart for developing cultures and leaders who are value-driven, people-centric and service-oriented. Previously served as a college soccer coach and has been employed as a teacher/professor and has served on the communication staff for several non-profit organizations. Now devotes her time to helping teams and groups to be at their best through workshops and public speaking. *Chapter 15*

Hamilton, Jody. Head Baseball Coach at West Jessamine High School. 2015 and 2001 State Champion at West Jessamine and Boyd Co. respectively. NHSCA Baseball Coach of the Year 2016, Kentucky Baseball Coach of the Year 2001, 2015. 15 Time Baseball Area and Regional Coach of the Year, KHSBCA HOF 1997, 916 wins (7th on all-time baseball win list). Drafted by Texas Rangers, signed with New York Yankees. Coached Golf, Football, Basketball and also served as Athletic Director. *Chapter 32*

Kesterson, Jean. Head Volleyball Coach, Cathedral High School, Indianapolis, Ind. (retired), Over 800 wins, 2015 National Champion, 8 State Championships, 12 Championship game appearances, 4 Gatorade Players of the Year, 17 All-Americans, Indiana Volleyball Hall of Fame. 2015 AVCA High School Coach of the Year and 2016 National High School Coach of the Year (NHSCA). *Chapters 2, 6, 22, and 29*

Koski, Bob. Head Varsity Track & Field Coach at Pojoaque Valley High School. Coached 33 New Mexico State Track & Field Champions, (individual and relay). 20 years certified experience as an educator and coach. Owner/Director of Koski Strength & Conditioning and author of the KSC Training Manual. *Chapters 29 and 35*

Ocampo, Aaron. Head Football Coach at Centennial High School, Las Cruces, NM, 2 State Runner-ups, 5 Semifinals, 10 Quarterfinals, 6 District Championships. Bachelor's Degree in Physical Education from the University of New Mexico and a Masters in Sport Administration from the University of New Mexico. Formerly Head Football Coach at Manzano High School in Albuquerque, NM from 2001 to 2011. Guided many players to All-State status and college football scholarships. *Chapter 25*

Sandlin, Daniel. Athletic Director East Jessamine High 2011-2017, Kentucky High School Athletic Director Association Board Member 2013-2017, Vendor Chair 2015-2017, President-Elect 2015-2017, 12th Region Athletic Director Vice President 2012-2013, President 2013-2016, Athletic Director of the Year 2015 and 2016, KHSAD Final Four 2015 and 2016. Jessamine County Great by Choice Award 2016. *Chapter 33*

Tucker, Cyrus (Cy). Former Head Coach Girls Soccer at South Oldham High School. 7 State Championships including 4 in a row. 390 wins (all-time leader in KY). 5 All-Americans and 5 Miss Kentucky Soccer recipients. State and Regional NSCAA Coach of the Year in 95, 96 and 98. Finalist for NSCAA National High School Coach of the Year in 01, 06 and 2010. 2015 National High School Coaches Association Coach of the year. Metro Athletic Director's High School Hall of Fame in 2004. Currently an assistant soccer coach at Oldham County High School. *Chapters 20 and 36*

Vanover, Karen. Teacher, Coach and Athletic Director at Lafayette High School. Kentucky's 1st female AD of a 4A school. AD for 20 years. Ten team and two individual state championships during tenure as AD. (NIAAA certified.) Coached Swimming and Diving, Cheerleading, Girl's Basketball, and Volleyball. State Swim Coach of the Year three times. Won many district and regional titles. Multiple winner of Regional AD of the Year and Kentucky State AD of the year with KHSADA, as well as National Runner-Up AAHPERD AD of the Year. Speaker at National NIAAA Conference and served on committees for the local, state and national associations. *Chapters 9, 15 and 22*

Wright, Kevin. Head Coach Girls Soccer, West Jessamine High. 2016 Girls State Champion, 1989 and1994 Boys State Runner-up (Montgomery Co.). Six state semifinals, Three Elite Eights, Seven Regional

Championships. Two Miss Kentucky Soccer recipients. 2016 State and National Finalist Coach of the Year (NSCAA). 2012 and 2015 NFHS Kentucky Coach of the Year. *Chapter 28*

Foreword

One of the most rewarding times of my career was the period I coached sport at a high school. It was a wonderful opportunity to shape young lives and create a few successful athletes but many more good people. As with all inexperienced coaches, I began in 'transactional' mode more concerned with the mechanics of practice than the young people I was coaching. I soon, however, found my natural inclination was 'transformational' coaching – paying attention to 'human beings' as well as 'human doings'. Two key lessons stayed with me through my career – 'it's not about me' and 'do no harm'.

It was Sir Alex Ferguson who made me realize that coaching a game is relatively easy, coaching a season is tough, and building a sustainable winning program is the most difficult coaching challenge of all. That is why I welcome this book and DeAngelo's intention of helping coaches build a successful high school program.

It is important that such a program is based on a definition of success that is aspirational but attainable for the context a particular coach works in – age, gender, level of competition. Often the pressure on coaches is defending this definition against the over-expectations of those surrounding the team. That is why in my work supporting high performances coaches I advise them to concentrate their efforts on the process of developing excellence and not on the outcome of the games. Easier said than done but it makes sense to put your efforts into what you can control rather than what you can't. Practise with relentless quality each day, and the wins will come to you.

Reviewing the book chapters, I was pleased to see that DeAngelo has recognized the importance of player and team mindset. My books underline the belief that: 'Success is a Mindset underpinned by physical, technical and tactical ability'. Talent and attitude are both required for success and coaches will occasionally come across players who have both. However, whereas talent levels can vary widely, shaping the attitude of players to the hard work of achieving excellence is far more under the control of the coach. One of my favorite sayings is that: 'It's not what you get from sport but who you become'. Sport challenges young people constantly and coaches can make a real contribution if they develop the character of their young people to face challenges with a fighter's mentality and not a victim's mentality.

From my experience, the barriers to successful high school coaching are over-coaching – losing simplicity and clarity through too much information and over-training – too many sessions and too long on the field. Avoid these, study this book and there is no reason why you can't develop excellent sports programs and build a rewarding coaching career.

I wish you good luck,

Bill Beswick.

Author *'Focused for Soccer'*

One Goal – the Mindset of Winning Soccer Teams

www.billbeswick.com

Table of Contents

About this Book

High school coaches are a dynamic multi-talented group. While the focus in my career has been soccer, I not unlike many of you, have been called upon to coach baseball, basketball, and archery. Administrators at that level understand that the need for quality leadership often trumps the need to find someone who has an impeccable pedigree in that particular sport.

It is with that in mind that this book has its roots. Not directed necessarily toward one particular sport (although many of my personal examples inevitably come from soccer), but for coaches who have varying backgrounds, levels of coaching experience, passions, and interest in building something special for their players and school.

Coaching any sport has common threads such as Leadership, Motivation, Selecting Your Team, Expectations, Challenges, Team Culture, etc. but what separates team sports from individual sports like Track and Field, Archery, Golf, Tennis, and others? In this book, all aspects of building a program either when working with individual athletes or teams are applicable. As a coach, reaching one athlete at a time is the fundamental building block of success. While we bring our team together to share ideas, strategies, and motivation, it is that ability to reach each player with trust, loyalty, respect, character and integrity that resonates.

Simply stated this is not a book about technique, tactics, strategy or plays. It is a leadership book to guide coaches through the everyday challenges, and through consistent decision making (doing the right thing), that coaching presents.

I wish you and your players the best on a wonderful journey.

1. The Coaching Interview, Are You Ready?

The score is 0-0, two minutes to go, and you have the ball at the halfway line. Can you maneuver through six or eight defenders, confidently maintaining possession, while the crowd roars, giving yourself a shot on goal to win the game? It's a lot of pressure, and only a prepared and skilled athlete can thrive in this situation.

What about when you're in position to score a coaching job, not just a goal? It's exactly the same type of pressure, with the stakes being higher when you want to win the job.

What's an AD or Athletic Committee looking for from an aspiring head coach in an interview? How can you leave it all on the table and give yourself the best opportunity of earning a better position?

Let's face it, a lot of coaching vacancies are filled by those with connections and big-time recommendations. In fact, some are filled before you even hear they're open. That being said, you'll never move forward if you don't take chances. So, how can you help yourself when the opportunity presents itself and you're in the interview?

How can I prepare? Do as much research as possible on the history and achievements of the school or club. Be able to talk about it comfortably. Develop practice questions to rehearse with someone to build your confidence. Make sure some of the questions are challenging and tough. You need to know how to answer, "Why are you leaving your current job?" or "Why wasn't your team successful?" Videotaping the practice interview may give you more insight on strengths, body language and areas of concern. *I've included a list of interview questions to consider.*

How do I set the stage with the greeting? When you enter the room, seek everyone out and greet them with a handshake while asking their name, leaning in and looking them in the eye. Let them know how honored you are to be there.

Are there right and wrong answers to the questions? Not really, just be yourself. Be consistent with questions dealing with discipline and how you would handle challenging situations. Stay with the question and don't wander off on some other subject. Trying to answer questions in a lofty way when that isn't really you will come through as fake.

How should I dress? Be professional looking when you show up. Remember, you'll be the face of the program and employers want a coach who shows and acts first class. Showing up casual and unkempt will be seen as a reflection of your personality and ultimately your coaching demeanor.

How do I talk/act? Stay focused, scanning the room and making eye contact with everyone as you answer questions. Make an effort to keep them involved by saying, "I know you've experienced that situation as well." Be respectful of everything you say and do. Refrain from talking ill of the previous coach. Only speak in terms of what you can do. Don't mention the challenges you had with your last team in a negative way, or make excuses.

How long should I speak about myself? Speak confidently and proudly with some humility mixed in. Be sure not to go on and on about what you've done. They're more concerned with what you can do for them. Mention those who've helped you such as assistant coaches, administrators, parents and outstanding players.

Should I have a presentation with my plans for the team? Absolutely! It shows you've done your homework and already have a detailed plan to start today with your new team. Include the team's logo throughout. The readiness and passion to start tomorrow is what they want. This is always impressive to interviewers.

What about my lack of success? Always be honest. If your success isn't or hasn't been where you wanted it to be, let them know your plans and what you plan to accomplish. Point out progress and successes that may not be apparent in the win-loss record. Let your passion to succeed shine. Be proud that you've worked hard, and continue to strive to achieve your goals.

What would indicate a lack of interest in me? You'll be able to get a real feel for interest in you, early in the interview. When interviewers start looking at each other waiting for someone else to ask a question or they don't seem to be paying attention, it may be a lack of interest. Another indicator may be the fact they're interviewing two candidates at the same time. This is a very uneasy situation, and they may be doing this to save time by running through candidates quickly. In my opinion, it's not a very professional thing to do and is an indication of how they run their sports program.

What about following up? Ask about the timeframe for filling the job, and when they plan on contacting those interviewed. It's always a good idea to call or email them the next day and thank them for taking the time to interview you. As you leave, walk around the room and shake hands again. Let them know if they have any questions they can contact you. If the deadline time passes with no contact, call them.

Is it a good idea to interview for several jobs at the same time? It can be a negative, especially since most AD's know each other and communicate frequently. They may feel you're job shopping and don't take theirs seriously. It can also be a distraction to be thinking of so many programs and keeping your information straight. Do your best to, at least, narrow it down to your top two.

Should I ask their vision of the new coach? Yes. It simply may not match what your expectations are, and it may not be possible to do so. If this is the case, let them know early.

Should I ask about the salary? Research the job first to see what it pays before the interview. You have to know if you can afford to make a job change from a personal standpoint. If you've done your research, you might say at the end of the interview, "I understand the salary for this position is _____. Is that correct?" If it's a negotiable salary, wait until an offer has been made or until they bring it up during the interview.

Interviews can seem contrived and certainly may miss something important that you feel is significant. Questions may have very little to do with who you are, and your ability to lead a team. If that's the case, share information you want the interviewers to know at the end of the interview.

Having been on both sides of the interview table, my recommendation is to just relax, be yourself and let the committee see you're the right person for the job. Allow your confidence to show, and be genuine in everything you say.

Nothing will guarantee you get the job, but think about all the attributes you want your players to have: Persistence, Character, Integrity, Loyalty, Work Ethic, Determination, and Relentlessness. Those are all the things you want to come across as you talk to the committee.

If this job doesn't work out, be persistent. Never lose that passion and continue to work toward your dream.

Here are a number of questions that may arise during a job interview.

1. What qualifies you for this job?
2. How will you deal with an angry parent after a game?
3. Define your coaching style in three words.
4. Describe a typical practice session for your team during the season.
5. Why are you leaving your current position?
6. Do you have expectations for your players? What are five?

7. What will give us an indication that you had a successful season?

8. Where does your coaching passion come from?

9. What have you used in the past to motivate your players?

10. Describe your best game and why. Your worst game/moment and why.

11. What role will your assistants have?

12. Your best player breaks a rule before a big game. How do you deal with it?

13. What are your strong coaching areas? Your areas of concern?

14. What do you hope your players take with them after they graduate?

15. How will you deal with your team after a heartbreaking loss?

16. What's your philosophy with respect to parents?

17. Several players complain about a certain player. How do you deal with it?

18. What specifically will you do to challenge your players?

19. How will you determine the leaders of your team?

20. What are three personal coaching goals you want to achieve?

21. What is your definition of character?

22. What are three words your colleagues would use to describe you?

23. Why should we hire you?

2. Why Not Build a Program?

As coaches, we often take over teams not knowing whether we'll be there next season or two years from now. That is the nature of our profession; the volatility of the coaching environment, better opportunities, changes in our own lives. At practice or during a game, we can become distracted by challenges or other aspects of our life, and do a less-than-ideal job with our team. It's easy to justify thoughts such as, "Well, I don't plan on being here next year so what does it matter?"

It does matter! To the players, their families, the school, and, more importantly, you! Everything you do is a reflection of your commitment and character. It doesn't matter if you'll be there tomorrow, the next day, or next week. What does matter is that you're there *right now*. You have a job to do, and you owe it to your players to do it the best way possible.

Build your program just as you would your house

A master carpenter had worked all his life and was ready to retire. His boss explained that he needed him to build one more house. Reluctantly, he agreed, even though his heart wasn't in it. During the job, he wanted to finish quickly, so he took shortcuts, used inferior materials, and generally provided shoddy workmanship. Eventually, he finished the house.

As he was gathering up his tools, his boss showed up to see the result. From the outside, the house looked magnificent, but the carpenter knew it would have problems and certainly wouldn't last as long as many he had built. When the boss paid him and shook his hand, he handed him the keys.

He said, "You've built so many beautiful houses for me I want to repay you as you retire with this house as a gift." Stunned, the carpenter thought, "If I had only known, I would have built it better."

So it is with us. We build our houses (programs) every day. We need to use the best resources, and do the most magnificent job possible so that they will last a long time. Those programs will always be a reflection of us, whether we're there one day, one season, or many years later.

Build the program so they can say, "We did it all ourselves without any help from the coach."

That's a pretty harsh and outrageous statement to some coaches. Especially when you've invested your heart, soul, and time into a program. But, as you think about that statement, it's the ultimate compliment. **It says you've given the players and the program the tools to stand by themselves.** True credit comes from within as a coach. Quality-focused coaches don't need people always complimenting them on what a great program and team they've developed. The results speak for themselves. It's okay to let others have and take credit for the program. Be proud of your work and the success you've allowed others to enjoy.

What are some of the keys to building a program?

1. **Passion** - Spread the fire for your mission!
2. **Engagement** - Load every helper you can find aboard your train!
3. **Salesmanship** - Use every opportunity to sell your program to anyone who is standing in front of you.
4. **Planning** - Develop a plan for what you want to accomplish with timetables and goals for each season.
5. **Expectations** - Start from day one and expect the best from your players.
6. **Resilience** - Be prepared to deal with setbacks; let nothing derail you.
7. **Work ethic** - Work every day with a fire!
8. **Avoidance of fool's gold** - Don't be comfortable with small victories; continue to work for the bigger prize.
9. **Encouragement/praise** - Everyone in your program - players, parents, administrators, and supporters - need encouragement and praise.
10. **Humility** - Step back and ask yourself, "Could they run it without me?" If so, you're doing your job, if not, you still have work to do.

Building a program starts the first day that you're announced as the new coach. You can't predict how long you'll be in one place, but you can never go wrong thinking that you'll be there for 20 years. That approach allows you the opportunity to build your dream and a positive program.

What will your program be known for, and stand for?

Without a doubt, building a program is a monumental task. As others see it, what will they notice? What do you envision? What will you be most proud of?

1. Development of players or winning at all costs?
2. Encouraging or threatening environment?
3. Positive character or embarrassing behavior?
4. Adhering to or breaking the rules?
5. Empowering or demeaning players?
6. Dealing with or screaming about mistakes?
7. High expectations or mediocrity?
8. Humility or boasting?
9. Passion or complacency?
10. Creativity or suppression?
11. Positive influence or trophies at all cost?
12. Shared leadership or dictatorship?

* * *

Indiana High School Volleyball Hall of Fame Coach Jean Kesterson shares her "Seven Steps to Developing a Successful High School Program".

1. Vision

Shared Vision: Coaches, Players, Parents, Administrators, and Community

- Develop a System
- Define roles: Coaches, Players, and Parents
- Develop a quality staff
- Develop a feeder program
- Don't reinvent the wheel
  - o Ask proven winners
  - o What do winners do that you can do in your program?

Setting Goals

- Develop 1-year, 3-year, and 5-year goals

- Look at Schedule
- Divide season into mini-seasons
- List practice goals
  - Practice your strengths
- List program/team/individual goals. Goals are SMART
  - Specific
  - Measurable
  - Attainable
  - Realistic
  - Timely

2. Pay the Price

- See Happy Players (important)
- Set high standards for the program
- No other team will out-work the volleyball team
  - Don't confuse activity with productivity
- EARN THE RESPECT OF THE SCHOOL
- Strong conditioning program
- Play volleyball
- Chalk talk sessions
- You need to work harder than your players

3. Coach Happy Players

- Fill the Circles
  - Mental
  - Social
  - Physical
  - Spiritual

4. Promote, Promote, Promote

- Make it important to play volleyball for your school
- RECRUIT. Get the best athletes to play volleyball
- Be visible. Get involved in everything at your school
- Belong to your state and national coaching associations

How?

- Fun environment
- Website
- Media guide
- Special events at games
- Camps
- Merchandise
- Highlight films/PowerPoint presentations
- Happy players and happy parents will promote for you

5. Communicate

With whom?

- Players
- Parents
- School/administration
- Community/feeder programs
- Media
- Alumni

How?

- Website
- E-mail
- Media guide
- Summer evaluation

- Player self-evaluation/teammate evaluation/1 on 1
- Don't burn any bridges
    - Making Cuts
    - The day before, on paper, players list five things they like about themselves. On the back side, players list five things they want to do in high school (no volleyball). Players make teams.
    - Ask good kids to stay in the program as statisticians/managers

Meetings

- 9th grade/Middle School meetings
    - The why is the most important thing
- Pre-season meetings with parents
- State Finals meeting

6. Establish Tradition

- How is your program branded?
- Establish tradition
- Goal circle
- Team meals
- Pre and post-match prayer
- Irish cheer
- Crazy Dress Up Day
- Senior night
- Parent night
- Dads decorating the bus
- Certain uniforms
- Pep band/music at games
- Seniors make banners
- Who sits where on the bus

- Seniors design uniform shirts

7. Have Fun

- Coaching is a precious gift
- Passion is contagious
- Coach/teach excellence

* * *

When you've taken care of the details while building your program, you'll see positive results. It takes time, so don't get discouraged. Use your power of being positive to create an environment where players feel encouraged to be creative, make mistakes, be challenged and just be themselves.

One day, standing on the sidelines, a smile will cross your face as someone takes time to congratulate you on your program. Or you will see an incident on the field, and suddenly realize that what you've been working for all these years came together in one wonderful moment.

Unlike the carpenter in our story, work hard every day and put your best work into your program. After all, you've been handed the keys.

3. Choosing Your Team

In today's world of ranking young players from 1-100, I'm often amazed at how a player (or players) ranked so high, can seem to underperform with their new team(s). Is it the ranking system, the coach, the dynamics of the team, pressure, or the player?

Many times, there's no way of knowing, but it is important to look at how coaches are evaluating players when they see them in action. Seeing them play once or twice, or relying totally on some outside ranking service can be a risky proposition. And when you get to college level, there's a lot to consider with scholarships and championships on the line. Making a mistake with a player or players can cost a program dearly.

While we may not be a college coach, I do believe the same principles apply at just about every level. Those choices will impact us in the same way, just not as much as for those in the public spotlight. Accordingly, we have to consider what's essential when evaluating players during tryouts.

What's at the top of your list when choosing your team?

1. Skill
2. Athleticism
3. Tactical Awareness
4. Attitude
5. Compatibility

Most of these attributed are fairly easy to evaluate through drills and activities. Likewise, you would recognize them if you saw them (even briefly) during a game with a player's former team.

Most coaches will admit they know a good player when they see one, but in what respect? There may be areas or traits that aren't exposed at tryouts, which only get surfaced when you see them in practice and games; by then it may be too late.

Successful programs look at

Adversity - Have you seen this player when times were tough, when he or she was behind in the score, their teammates weren't performing, their own game was off that day? How did they react? Can you live with that? Can your team?

Character - How do they respond when things are going well or not? How do they treat their teammates? Are they a team player, or only concerned with themselves?

Integrity - Are they a player of their word? Do they stand up for what they believe in? Will they always tell you the truth? Can they be trusted?

Academics - Are they responsible in the classroom? What's their past history with respect to grades and discipline issues at school? Will you spend a lot of time keeping them eligible? Work ethic must be present in the classroom.

Training - What type of work ethic do they have? Are they a driven player, or will you have to motivate them every minute of every day? Are they capable?

Criticism/critique - Are they able to take any suggestions/ideas you, or your assistants, have with an open mind and a willingness to improve? How do they respond with body language, and verbal responses?

How can you evaluate these traits?

During tryouts, set up challenging games and activities where each player is:

1. Paired or teamed with a player or players of lesser ability.

2. Playing a game where their team is always a player down.

3. Paired or teamed with a player or players of greater ability.

4. Playing a game where their team is behind by one with little time on the clock, and they are the only player who can score. Or they're the only player who can defend the only player who can score for the other team.

5. Unable to shoot, only pass.

6. Only allowed to defend. Hops out of the game when their team has the ball.

7. The only player allowed to talk, or not, on their team.

8. The only player on their team that has to touch the opposite goal or end line when the ball is lost before hustling back and defending.

9. The only player that runs when their team loses. Or the rest of the team runs when they make a mistake or miss a shot.

Seeing how they respond will tell you what you need to know, and the best avenue to take in developing their abilities to respond under pressure, as well as their technical skills. There are many more activities that put players in pressure situations where their true Character shines through. It requires no more effort from you. Everything I've mentioned, and all the ideas you have, will also expose Skill, Athleticism, Tactical Awareness, Attitude, and Compatibility.

Planning a great tryout session is the key to selecting the best players for your team. Understanding where they stand now with the areas you feel are important will allow you to assist them to become better players. It will also give you a strong idea of who performs best under pressure during key moments. Tryouts should expose more than outstanding skills; they should expose the individuals who you can count on when times are tough.

As a coach, you know the tough times are coming.

Field Player Assessment

Technical-Ball Skills

1. Long distance passing/Shooting (Accuracy and Power)

2. Passing (Either foot)

3. Dribbling, Individual Moves

4. Heading, (Defensive and Attacking)

5. Receiving (First touch)

6. Striking the ball (Volleying)

Tactical-Decision Making

1. Moving without the ball (Understanding of Space)

2. Switching the point of Attack/Field Vision (Head up)

3. Willingness and Anticipation to win 50/50 balls

4. Confidence/Creativity to take players on

5. Confident decision to pass, dribble or shoot

6. Individual defending (Marking space or opponent)

Physicality-Athleticism

1. Strength with the ball (Shielding)

2. Strength in the Air (Jumping, Timing, Winning balls out of the air)

3. Speed (more than 20 yards)

4. Explosiveness (Less than 10 yards)

5. Endurance and Stamina

6. Willing to stick in and win the ball

Psychological/Emotional-Intangibles

1. Communicator/Assertive/Positive

2. Leadership-Ability to pick others up/Willing to speak up

3. Teamwork-Ability to bring teammates together

4. Work Ethic-Determined/Tireless/Driven

5. Willingness to accept new ideas and grow

6. Sportsmanship-Respects opponents and officials

Goalkeeper Assessment

Technical

1. Handling low shots (on ground or bounce)

2. Handling high shots (reaction/anticipation/jumping ability)

3. Body Position (footwork, hands ready, always alert)

4. Distributing the ball (passing/rolling)

5. Punting (accuracy/power/distance/consistent)

6. Goal Kicks (accuracy/power/distance/consistent)

Tactical

1. Commanding and Setting defenders in dead ball situations

2. Taking charge in the back/Communication/Field Vision

3. Anticipation of winning loose balls (close to the goal)

4. Confidence on pass back and uses foot skills to distribute the ball

5. Clear/Decisive decision to come off the line or hold position

Physicality-Athleticism

1. Strength with the ball (Holding on to, and covering, the ball)

2. Strength in the Air (Jumping, Timing, Parrying)

3. Quickness/Reflexes-Hand Eye coordination

4. Explosiveness (Less than 10 yards)

5. Winning 1v1 and breakaway battles

Psychological/Emotional

1. Communicator/Encourager/Positive

2. Leadership-Willingness to speak up

3. Teamwork-Reminds team it's a 90-minute battle, stays positive.

4. Work Ethic-Determination/Tireless

5. Student of the game-Willing to listen and hungry to learn new ideas/concepts

6. Sportsmanship- Respects every opponent/official

4. Selling Your Program

Have you ever looked in the stands, as your team is warming up, and felt discouraged that there are not more fans there? Often it's just the parents or extended families that show up. Why does this happen? It's tough not to take it personally, especially when your team has worked so hard during the week and over the course of a season. Surely they deserve better?

Our main focus will always be to coach, but can we do anything to help alleviate the lack of support? While it may take extra effort on our part, and even be uncomfortable for some, I believe there is.

There can be many reasons our stands are so empty

1. Families are too busy
2. Too many other options/obligations crowd games out
3. The team isn't very good
4. People aren't aware of your schedule/team
5. Ticket prices are too high
6. The weather is uncomfortable

We could go on, and I'm sure you could add to our list, but does this kind of knowledge help us with getting fans out to watch our games? Maybe, if we know what we're competing against.

Football and Basketball seem to be the big draws, and I feel certain it has to do with the fact that many have played each sport, or know someone who did. Indeed, a lot of people are familiar with those sports from when they grew up. They also tend to be social events with tailgating or a 'who's who' social gathering where people can see and be seen. Do these sports give us a hint of how we can get the fans to our games? I think so.

It all begins with selling your program. Even though you're in the middle of an undefeated season or playing in the state tournament, there are no guarantees, so you can't sit back and expect fans to come out.

We live in a society where fans must be entertained or enticed to come to the game. If you attend major college or pro games, it can sometimes feel as if the entertainment overshadows the game. At every timeout or halftime, your attention is turned to the giant scoreboard, dance team, cheerleaders, or celebrity guests to keep you engaged. Can we afford to do that? Probably not to such a degree, but we can certainly do more.

How can you get creative with a low budget?

Free Tickets - What if you gave out a number of free game tickets to students throughout the day with the hook of having a prizedraw for a big gift at halftime? It may cost you some gate money tonight, but may also create interest as the season progresses. Plus you'll make more money on friends who join them and on concessions. The key is the giveaway. It has to be something desirable.

Gold/Silver Fan Membership - Establish admission standards based on contributions, either through money or volunteering, for those who support your program. Former players and their families could be included as well. You could recognize them at select games.

Kids Play Area/Games - Are you willing to set up kids' games or areas for the little ones to play and have fun? Parents would probably come if their little ones can have fun also. Promote this idea with your boosters.

Halftime honors - Can you make an effort at halftime to honor past teams, military personnel, youth teams, etc. When someone is honored, they certainly bring their families with them.

Entertainment - What demographics are you're trying to get to the game? Vary the music and entertainment based on different groups for different nights. Every night should have a theme and activities to match.

Tailgating - Can you establish a tradition at your games where the fans consistently want to tailgate over the course of a season? You could have cooking and grilling contests, etc. Let the parents run with this idea.

Players - Is there a way your players can go as a group or small groups to promote your game or season to businesses in the area? They could also visit elementary and middle schools creating an interest, and even conduct clinics.

You – Join, or be a member of, civic groups in your town. Ask to speak at different events or meetings. Be as involved as time allows in your community. Talk about and sell your program to everyone you meet. Create a desire or curiosity for people to come watch your team play.

Social Media - Use this to your advantage concerning special events for the game each night. If you don't have time, let one of the parents or other students do it. Every game should be highlighted on Twitter, Facebook, Team Webpage, Instagram, etc.

Pep Band/Cheerleaders/Dance team/Mascot - You should be able to have a least one of these at every game. Do your best to sell it to the sponsors/coaches of these groups. It's a great time for exposure for them and certainly helps generate excitement for your game.

I agree that your main job (and what you were hired to do) is coach your team, but there is so much more you can do. **You're the face of the program.** Your strength may not lie in carnival-tone barking to get fans to attend your games, but you can lead in other ways. Simply making suggestions and recommendations to booster members and parents who may be more suited to this task will help. They can do the barking for you.

Selling you program today simply on its own merits, regardless of how successful it may be, isn't enough anymore. Recognizing that, and starting today to build fan interest in your community will benefit your team in more ways than attendance. Those who show up with children, and see the atmosphere, will want them to attend your school.

Working to see that our players and team get what they deserve will always be our responsibility. Looking up in the stands and seeing smiling fans should be one of our goals.

5. That Championship Vision

We all want to know how we can prepare our teams and build that hunger for a championship.

We're aware it takes commitment and determination from the coaching staff and our players to be in a position to make a championship dream a reality. But is there more we can do?

Is there a way we can relate the ultimate victory to every learning modality – visual, kinesthetic and auditory – so our players can see, touch, hear and smell what it's like to experience a championship game before they've ever been there?

Remember, some players may have never experienced a championship. By painting a mental picture every day, in practice, using one of the images or situations listed below, we can build a foundation that players can relate to, and, ultimately, provide them with a sense of what a championship is like.

Attend/watch a championship game/meet - Take your team to the title game. Sit as close to the action as possible. Let them see the skill, determination, and adversity involved to compete at this level. Often, players don't observe other teams' games or watch high-level games on TV, only their own. They need to see how top teams warm-up, prepare and play in a championship setting. Ask questions about what they see.

- How are those teams different from us? How are they the same?

- What player most resembles you and your style of play?

- What words describe what it would take to reach the championship?

Smell/Visualize the game -With your team seated at practice, have them close their eyes and just smell the field, the surroundings, and imagine their best game as an individual and/or as a team. With a soccer game, for example, have them visualize a game when they had that perfect pass, perfect goal, perfect save, or perfect defensive move in their best moment. Lead them to another place where they fought through adversity as an individual and or as a group with all they had, and how special it was.

- What did it take?

- How did you feel?

- Why did you do it?

Hold the trophy - Bring the biggest trophy possible to practice and have the players pass it around. If you've already won a championship, bring that trophy. Let them take selfies with it, and/or as a group or team. Have players rotate taking it home each night. Sit it on the sideline during practice where everyone can see it. You might have everyone touch it before or after practice as a reminder of their goal. Be sure to explain that trophies, while beautiful, are just a symbol of the dedication and efforts of a team.

- Can you imagine celebrating our championship with the trophy?

- How would you want players 10 years from now to remember you?

- Can a trophy tell the whole story of your dedication?

Hear the fans - With no distractions, have the players close their eyes and imagine the roar of their fans as the team fights to win a championship, and the deafening noise when they win the game. Imagine fans storming the field. Bring in recorded crowd cheering if you need. Build that feeling of playing in a packed stadium or arena.

- Who did you hear in the crowd? How do you think they felt?

- Can you look around and see the stands full of fans?

See your parents/relatives - Ask your players to think of their parents and all they've sacrificed to get them to this point. Imagine seeing them in the stands, running down on the field when they win that championship, or when they get home, and all the hugs and tears. While they're always proud of everything a player does, this would be a special gift to them and the other parents from a player and their teammates.

- What would this mean to your parents or guardians?

- What would it mean to you?

Feel the pain/satisfaction of working so hard despite setbacks -
Winning a championship won't be easy, and there are no guarantees. There may be setbacks, but always work toward, and stay focused on, that

goal – one practice and one game at a time. Show your team that they'll be better players and people for the journey. Knowing they've pushed themselves all season and left it all on the field is a must in a championship season.

- Have you achieved a goal despite challenges? What was it?

- Are you willing to give more effort?

- Can you encourage others to do the same?

- How would you deal with a terrible game? Injury?

Ask players to see their teammates - The joy of this journey with others is what makes it so special. Everyone has contributed and sacrificed. It's amazing to see teammates so supportive of each other. Working so hard, encouraging each other, and celebrating with those who've seen through the tough times will be a memory of a lifetime. Teammates count on each other to play their best every night. A player needs to learn that their skill may not be the same every night, but effort has to be. Ask your players:

- Who on our team would you be most happy for?

- Who has encouraged/pushed you the most?

Challenge your players to play for someone else - The feeling of playing the game and being inspired by someone else will make it worth more. They need to understand that others have struggled or have challenges in life they may never face. Put the game up for them. Have them visit those individuals before the game to reaffirm what their true values are, and to strengthen their determination to play their best. Then make a point for them to visit soon after the game.

- Who would they play for?

- Why are they an inspiration?

Ask them, "How far have you have progressed?" - Can individuals recall and remember the player they were *before* today, and who they *are* today. Working for a championship has given them new purpose and a sense of responsibility. Very few players can say they won a championship. It's time for them and their teammates to be on that list. Have your players picture their team giving the effort of a lifetime.

- What have they learned about themselves this season?
- Are they a different person/player? How?

Guest speaker - Bring in one or more of your former players who have played on a championship team to speak with the team, if possible. You could also bring in a player or more who, while they didn't win a championship, benefitted greatly by challenging themselves every day. It may also be wonderful to bring in someone who has overcome insurmountable odds to accomplish everything in their life. Their story of never giving up, and fighting for what they have, may be the inspiration your team needs.

- What message did your players hear?
- How was it important to them?
- How does it relate to a championship?

Pictures/Words - Give every player a piece of paper and marker. Have them write or draw a word or picture describing what they believe it takes to win a championship. Then, have the team decide which words or pictures will be used every day, on the road to a championship. Have them create a poster to see, and touch, every day before practice as a reminder that for practice to be successful those words or pictures must be achieved. Remember, these were generated and selected by the team (you may want to use them all), not you.

- Why did they select that word/picture?
- What will they have to do to make the poster possible?
- How can they be reminded of these poster values every day?

Puzzle/Team Photo - Take one of your team pictures and have it made into a puzzle, one with a lot of pieces. On a night out, when the team is out enjoying a dinner, break out the puzzle without letting them know what it is and have them put it together. Hold back a few pieces and after it's all put together with what they have, ask a few questions.

- Why do they need the other parts of the puzzle?
- How could the missing parts relate to their team and a championship?

- What will they do if they're missing a few parts of the team this season?

While most of us would agree that our teams need to focus on one game at a time, I believe you can also build the image of a championship along the way.

We often expect our players to want the same things we want and know how to achieve it. Unfortunately, without our guidance, our team can get off track and lose its way. Players need a vision of what a championship run could mean to them individually and as a team. They need a vision of what it would take to get to that level, and what it would take to ultimately be challenged every day in every aspect of the game.

It's up to us, as coaches, to paint that championship picture with a passion using every resource available. Bring it to life and build that hunger for your team!

6. Building Your Team

When you conduct tryouts for your team, do you use criteria or an evaluation form? Or do you feel comfortable without one, knowing from experience what to look for with respect to a player's technique, tactics, and their physical and psychological attributes?

I've never been involved in a legal battle over not keeping a player, but I believe it's a good idea to have a record of each player and their ranking.

My assistants and I discuss two key questions after evaluating a player with respect to making our varsity squad:

1. With their current skills, will it be possible for us to put this player in a game?

2. Is there sufficient time in their career, to develop into a contributing player?

If the answer is no to either or both, our decision is clear. We can't keep them.

At the high school level, especially with the varsity, you have to scrutinize your selection and player-development processes very diligently. If a player is a junior or senior and hasn't developed, one of three things may have happened:

1. We made a mistake in keeping this player as a freshman and certainly as a sophomore. We were hoping. Never deal in hope.

2. The player wasn't motivated enough to improve. They were just on the team for the social aspect and never worked on their game.

3. We didn't have (or made) the time to work with this player. Always look in the mirror and ask yourself, "Did I do everything possible?"

Either way, it's time to make the right decision. Let them go.

With freshmen and sophomores, the decision is easier. If you need players, you can justify keeping a less-skilled candidate in an effort to develop them. If they have a great work ethic and attitude, it's easier to keep them. **The term "potential" often comes up with young players, and I dislike it. I always use "capable of."** For these two grades, you still have the junior varsity team where they can play if it's needed for them to develop.

That being said, if it's obvious they probably aren't going to improve, don't keep them. You're just delaying the inevitable.

Players want to play and you, as a coach, wouldn't want them being content sitting on the bench. It does the player and their parents an injustice to keep them if you can't put them in a game. They'll become disgruntled, along with their parents, because they believed that issuing them with a uniform meant they were going to play. It is better not to keep them, even if they hate you for a day or a week, than it is for them to hate you for a season and destroy the attitude of your team.

We have open tryouts, utilizing various activities for our veterans and new players. For the first three days, we bring in our middle school players only, usually Wednesday, Thursday, and Friday. Then the next week, beginning on Monday, we bring our grade 9-12 players in to complete the group, including those who may be new. In our State, only grades 9-12 are eligible to play varsity, and no 11th or 12th graders can play JV, or practice with the younger players. I explain to the group that our staff will be evaluating them for these first eight days and we'll sit down and talk with each of them on Friday with respect to whether they will make the team or not.

Didn't we talk to her on Friday about not making the team?

One year, after the first week of practice/tryouts, and selecting our team, we told those who made it to come back on Monday. As they arrived to put their gear on and were talking, I noticed a player to whom we had explained that she didn't make the team. I asked my assistant to be sure, because this had never happened before, and she affirmed what I thought. When I approached the player, I reminded her that we had talked and we couldn't keep her at this time. She told me that her grandmother didn't believe her when she broke the news. I asked where her grandmother was, and she pointed to a car at the edge of the field. I said I'd explain it to her. The conversation went well, and her grandmother understood. An uneasy moment without question, but all part of coaching.

Players' Roles

After you've selected your team, do you and your staff meet with each player explaining what you see as their role, what they do best, where they need to improve, and tell them how proud you are that they're on the team?

Players will comfortably gravitate toward an image of what they see their capabilities being. As a coach, you have to share your vision and expectation of what your players can become and how you need them to play. It's important to explain that being uncomfortable at times is a sign of growth, lasting only a while until it becomes a habit. If we don't challenge each player and take them to a new level, we're not doing our jobs.

Getting that Commitment

It's also vital that you have a detailed plan of practice/game schedules/activities/trips, etc. to share with each player. You need to ask, "Do you have any conflicts with our plans?" There will be times they aren't sure, so have them take the plan home for their parents to review. You can also review this at your first parent meeting. There's nothing worse than a player coming to you and saying they can't be at a game or some other event because of previous commitments with the family. They have to know that other than an emergency their commitment is to this team and their teammates.

* * *

Volleyball Coach Jean Kesterson who has over 800 wins, coached 17 All-Americans and 4 Gatorade players of the year, once again shares her experience and wisdom; this time with regard to building a team and culture.

Building a team/program culture

- Defined shared values
    - Everyone can agree on the items that the team will value
    - Work hard every practice
    - Be on time
    - Do what is best for the team
    - Everyone has the right to an opinion
    - Positive body language in every drill, every match
    - It's not about you; it's about the team's success
    - Everyone has value

- Set stretch goals
    - Win a state championship

- o Be ranked in the top five nationally
- o Win a national championship
- o Earn the Team Academic Award

- Know your Generation
  - o Generation Z born 1995 to now
  - o These are our players
  - o They need to know if the end is worth it

- What makes them so different?
  - o First generation 100% digital native
  - o Crave for constant and quick feedback
  - o Comfortable talking face-to-face
  - o Looking for stability
  - o Gen Z sees sports more as a health tool
  - o Will not tolerate mistreatment or discrimination, especially group punishment
  - o Shorter attention span, about 8 seconds

- How should you coach Gen Z?
  - o Talk to them
  - o Be positive
  - o Know your sport
  - o Get input from them, better buy-in
  - o Listen to them

- Know How to Motivate
  - o Autonomy
  - o Don't micromanage
  - o They will make mistakes

- o Coach on the average
- o Tell them how to correct their errors without negatives

* * *

Building a team takes courage

You'll have to make decisions that may be uncomfortable with respect to telling a player he or she didn't make the team. I always leave a player with, "You're welcome to come back again next season for tryouts." As we talk, we also highlight the attributes we saw while they were with us, like effort, hustle, determination, etc. Add something like, "At this time, with your skill level, we just couldn't see playing you in a game, and we know you wouldn't be happy just sitting on the bench."

Thankful for a coach I never played for...

Before I ever entertained the idea of coaching I was a player just like so many of you. I played my first two years at a small college, and it was a comfortable setting, but it was time to continue my education at a larger school. The fever was still there to play, and I ended up trying out for the team. It was clear that I didn't have the skill level to compete, but I wouldn't go away.

Finally, during the pre-season, the coach called me into his office. In the most heartfelt manner, he let me know that there just wasn't room for me on the team. He spent 15 minutes highlighting all the attributes I had shown that would make me a success in any career I chose. As I left, I wanted to cry, but couldn't because of all the great things he had said. Ironically, 20 years later I would end up coaching, and pattern that same style of talking with players after this wonderful man.

I know many coaches post a list of who made the team and justify it because of time restraints, but I don't agree with that policy. It gives the impression of a coach who doesn't want to see or deal with those players who weren't good enough to make the team. Think for a moment if it was you who tried out for the team. Would you want to look at a cold, posted list on a wall for all to see? Step up as a coach and look every player in the eye who gave up their time to try out for your team. Have the courage to tell them why they didn't make it. A coach looked me in the eye and made a huge difference in my life. It takes character to do the right thing.

7. Player Expectations

As I sat nervously on the bus, looking at my watch, my thoughts were about the team we were about to play. They were a top-five team, and we'd need everyone to play a perfect game to give ourselves a chance to win. But where was Krystal? She was our senior defender, and the key to shutting down the opposition's attack. I learned quickly that she thought we played later in the day and had overslept. She would be here in 15 minutes, but that was too late, and as a senior she knew our expectations. Of all the players on our team, she would have been at the bottom of my list as the one who might put herself and the team in this position. We left without her.

A moment like this demands consistent leadership from you. In the pre-season and during the season, we talk with our players about what is expected of them. I've included our expectations list, which is read and signed by our players and one of their parents.

One of those expectations is that everyone must ride the bus as a team to all away games. If they don't, they have to sit on the bench and watch the game, or sit the next game out if they fail to make it. In this incident, we had to start a 9th grader in the back as one of our primary defenders. She had very little experience. Even though she and the team did all they could, we lost in a huge way. You could tell our team wasn't mentally sharp due to the situation.

The player who sat out is one of my all-time favorite players: very athletic and highly skilled with a truly wonderful, supportive family. It's a little easier to hold those accountable you believe deserve it, but expectations have no favorites. Once you decide what those expectations are, everyone must abide by them, and you must make sure you follow through.

Some expectations are required through the school or association that your team plays for, such as abstaining from drugs and alcohol. However, you must decide what other behaviors you can live with or without. Do your best to limit the list. If you feel you can't enforce an expectation, or it's just trivial and not that important, don't include it. I suggest allowing the team to assist in setting your expectations if at all possible. This gives them ownership and a greater understanding of what's necessary for a team to be successful. And, honestly, they'll be more likely to follow them.

Expectations define your philosophy with respect to character and integrity for the team and how you'll handle situations that require action.

However, just because you develop a consequence for a certain expectation, don't expect that to work for every incident. There will be extenuating circumstances in some situations that will test your ability to act fairly. I always tell the players that I'll be fair, but I can never be equal. The key is to be as consistent as possible, show no favoritism, and in moments of compromise explain it to the team.

On another occasion, I got a phone call that one of our players had just broken her ankle over the weekend in an annual student football game! I was astonished because this was our senior goalkeeper. I had always tried to make a point to our players to stay away from this game. It involved players who weren't really athletes just looking to have a good time. It was a recipe for disaster, but I had always trusted my players to make good decisions, rather than include them in my list of expectations.

The accident happened as we were preparing for the District Tournament. At our level of play, we really didn't have a true backup, and this was one of the best teams our school had assembled since the start of the program. Turns out it was a freak accident but my heart immediately went to how bad she must feel, especially since this was her senior year.

I visited her and her family in the hospital. The doctors had to put screws in her ankle, but the prognosis was good with no long-term effects. I was thrilled she was able to be with us as we ended up winning the regional tournament. Our new goalkeeper, who had primarily played softball and basketball, had great hands. With her in the frame, we advanced to the final eight of the state tournament, eventually losing 1-0.

Expectations aren't always about being on time, showing respect, and following the rules. They are, as in the example above, about making good decisions with respect to yourself and the team.

In addition, coaching isn't only about technique, tactics, winning, and losing. It's about being able to guide your team through issues and challenges. Consistent leadership in those areas is the key to the team's success. After all, life lessons are more important than making a great save, or scoring a goal. The team is a reflection of your values, and that's always going to be evident to those watching them play.

Player Expectations

We will always conduct ourselves with dignity and class, on and off the field, knowing that we represent our family, our school, and our community.

Physical examinations must be completed by a physician each year on a State Association Form issued by the school and turned into the coach before being allowed to practice or play.

Uniforms and warm-ups are the responsibility of the player, once in their possession, until they turn it in to the coach. They will be worn **only** to our games or school the day of our game if designated by the team or coach.

Lost or damaged uniform items due to negligence will be replaced by the player. **Complete uniforms and warm-ups must be turned in at the banquet.**

Players who have not paid team fees, school activity fees, past due fees from soccer or any other sport, or other fees deemed necessary by the team or school will not be issued a uniform or allowed to practice or play.

Players missing practice the day before a game will not be allowed to play in that contest, but must accompany the team to the game, and make that time up before being allowed to play. (JV players practicing or playing "club soccer" may be **eligible** to play under the coach's discretion, as long as they have notified the coach in advance).

Players who miss two consecutive practices without notifying a coach will be subject to dismissal from the team.

Players missing practice due to family vacations, and other circumstances during the season will make up lost time with extra conditioning and ball work before or after regular practice.

Players are required to ride the bus/van with the team to away games. Players who are late, and miss the bus, will not be allowed to play in that contest.

Bullying/Hazing will not be tolerated, and be dealt with through the school's handbook. Notify a coach or an adult immediately if you witness this happening.

Drug and alcohol use will not be tolerated, and dealt with through our school's drug policy procedures.

Players must be passing all classes to play or practice.

Players conduct in school including tardiness, respectfulness, and absenteeism will be subject to review by the coaches and Athletic Director.

Players absent from school on the day of a game will not be allowed to play unless approved by the Athletic Director and or Principal.

Players receiving a "red card" will sit out the mandatory next game or games with respect to the State Associations' Guidelines, and are subject to dismissal from the team depending on the offense.

I have read and understand the expectations Date _____

_____

Player Parent or Guardian

8. Bringing Your Team Together

Have you ever considered using team building activities? Many coaches I've talked with are amazed at their team's ability to work together and accomplish seemingly impossible challenges, and I have to agree!

That's why we've always implemented them in our program before the season begins. There is simply nothing like taking your team somewhere, and assigning group challenges for which they have to depend on each other (sound familiar?) to accomplish a task they've never done before.

Some of the benefits of team building activities are:

1. Leaders are easily recognized.
2. Dynamics of working together are exposed.
3. True competitors are obvious.
4. A willingness to help each other is seen.
5. New talents are highlighted.
6. Everyone escapes from the pressure of the game.
7. Veteran players assist younger players.

We're fortunate in our area to have a college with a high and low ropes course. Two years ago, we took our team to the high course, several years after completing the low course. The players loved it. Everyone participated and finished the course, with their teammates cheering them on. We had players who were expert climbers and were fearless in everything they did. It was a talent that would never have been seen, had we not done the course. Did I mention the coaches completed the course as well?!

We've always made a point to do a few activities when we traveled to team camps in the summer as well. I've included a list of several collected from other coaches and resources. Tarp, Paper Plates, String Toss, Minefield, Paper Chains and Team Puzzle are a few of my favorites. I still have a "Chain" created by my team for me from team camp several years ago. The ones they made for each other were very special, and we all had fun making them. Memories made doing these activities last a lifetime, and the benefits far outweigh any time taken away from practice.

Team building activities create new bonds among teammates never seen before and carry over into the season. The positive effect can't be measured. Go ahead – do something fun with your team. Besides bringing your team closer together, they will see a side of you they've never seen before. It's okay.

Team building activities

Rope knot game - Divide into two or three teams. Have team members evenly spaced along a rope that has a single knot tied at each point where someone is standing, (7 members, 7 knots, etc.). Each player must have one hand on the rope (same one) at all times. The object is to – *one at a time* – untie your knot and step through the rope, and then the next person goes. The first team to untie their knots and have a straight rope wins.

Rope challenge - Use a large rope ½" to 1" thick (a tug of war rope works well). Have half of the team sit down on one side of the rope and the other half on the other side, opposite sides facing each other. Everyone grabs the rope with both hands, alternating hands with the person across from you. The challenge is for the whole team to stand up at the same time while holding the rope with both hands. Only one designated person is allowed to speak. Feet must begin flat on the ground or floor.

Hula hoop challenge - The team makes a circle with arms locked together or holding hands. If you have a large group, you may want to split them into groups of 8 or so and have a competition. Coach unlocks two players' arms or hands and places a hula-hoop between them, placing their hands or arms back together through the hoop. The object of the game is to pass the hula-hoop around the circle by stepping or passing through it until the hoop has traveled all the way around and back. If anyone breaks hands or arms, the team must start over.

Off the floor - Sit down across from a partner with knees bent, feet flat on the floor, and hold onto each other's wrists or forearms. The object is to work together to attempt to raise your and your partner's backside barely off the floor for 10 seconds. Progress to groups of 3, 4, 6, 8, and then the whole team. Make the time shorter as the group increases.

Pyramids - Have a large group of players jogging around in a designated area. Coach yells out a number, and the players must get with a group of that number and build a pyramid. Anyone left out must do something silly (donkey kick, I'm a star, sing a song, etc.). If you have an even number of players, yell an odd number. For odd numbers of players, yell an even number.

Paper plates - As the title of the game suggests, you need paper plates (oh, and some tape). Preferably duct tape, and you may want to design the plate to resemble your sport's ball. Or you can copy an image and print the number of plates needed on thick paper.

Each player puts tape on the back of their plate and has someone stick it on their back. After everyone is ready, all players who also have a Sharpie (Sharpies should be the same color so no one can figure out who wrote what), walk around the room and write something positive or flattering about that player on their plate. You can encourage them to write something positive about the sport they play with respect to skill, etc. I have them tape the plate to their locker as a reminder of what they mean to each other.

Toss the string - Start with a spool of yarn. Team members form a circle and coach, or a player, begins the game by holding the end of the yarn, offering a little-known fact, or a commitment with respect to the team that they will do this year. They then toss the ball of yarn across the circle to another player who repeats. Each player holds onto the string, creating a web throughout the activity. You can repeat the activity in a different sequence or start all over again, only this time say something positive about the player you're tossing it to with respect to your sport. In the end, with everyone holding onto the string, make a point to remind everyone how connected they all are, and that it will take everyone doing their job for the team to be successful.

Paper chains - Cut pieces of construction paper of different colors into 1" by 9" strips. Have plenty of markers of different colors available along with several rolls of tape. Each player begins by writing their name and squad number on a strip of paper (they may decorate it also), before taping it together to form a loop and passing it to the person to their right. When you receive a player's loop, write something positive about them, decorate it, and add it to their necklace by taping it together. Then hand it to the player to your right. Continue around the circle until everyone has a nice necklace or chain with lots of compliments.

Tires - Divide the team up into groups of 8 or 9 and see if they can all stand with at least one foot on a car tire at the same time and sing a 30-second song.

Cross the river - Use a 30-yard grid. Divide your team into equal groups of 8 or 9. Each group receives three towels (Large bathroom towels or inexpensive small rugs work well). Set up an area with cones or lines for a start and finish line. The object is for all group members to travel across the grid (river) without anyone falling off the towel. Lay the towels down and walk across them, moving towels from back to front to progress across the river. Towels can only go in one direction, and the first team across wins. If anyone falls off, the team must start at the beginning.

Form shapes - Divide into two or three teams. Each team's members get evenly spaced along their rope, holding onto it, blindfolded. Coach yells out shapes (square, triangle, etc.) for the team to form. Progress to octagon, hexagon, numbers, etc. Have a time limit, after which all team members open their eyes to see how accurate their shape is.

Standing on a towel or handkerchief - Divide into 2 or 3 teams. Use a kitchen towel (small) or handkerchief. The object is for each team member to get at least one foot touching the towel and one foot up in the air for at least 5 seconds. The first team to do it wins. Players are allowed to stack on top, or step on, other players' feet that are on a towel.

Team puzzle - Send your team picture to a website that creates puzzles from pictures. When you get it back, get the team together and tell them they're putting a puzzle together without letting them know it's a team picture. Bring popcorn and soft drinks to make it enjoyable. You may want to have the website add a header or footer which says, "Championship Season" (as a hint of what you feel they can accomplish). Deliberately hold back two or three pieces, or more, as an example of what happens when all the pieces of a season (commitment, dedication, etc.) don't come together.

Tarps - Buy several small tarps (5X5 or 5X7) at your local discount store. Divide your players into several groups. Make sure the groups are large enough to barely fit on the tarp when all are standing up. The object of the game is for the team to turn the tarp completely over while all the team members stay on. If someone falls off, or steps off, they have to start over. The first team to do it wins.

Minefield - A large indoor area works best, but this can be conducted outside on your field. Use cones, balls, water bottles, hurdles, etc. to create an obstacle course of mines in your empty space. Divide the squad up into two or four teams. Within the teams, have them pair up with someone who will attempt to cross the minefield and one who will guide them from the opposite sideline. All who are going should line up on one end, and those directing them should spread out on the opposite sideline. Divide the field down the middle so those crossing have to stay on their side. When one player starts, let them get five or six steps away before the next one goes. If they go out of bounds, they start over. You may want to have one obstacle where the whole team has to start over if it gets touched. Did I mention that the players crossing the minefield have blindfolds on? Headbands make great blindfolds. When all the members make it to the other side, have them switch with their partner and complete the course coming back. The first team to get all their players across is the winner. Play the game one more time but let the teams decide what they will do differently and incorporate it the second time around. Players crossing the course may not carry another player or hang on to them. The fun begins when all players are on the course at the same time with all their partners yelling.

Ski board relays - For this activity, you'll need to invest in and build some equipment, but it's easily attained and built.

Supplies needed:

- Four 8-foot 2x6 boards
- 120 feet of 3/8" polypropylene rope
- Vinyl Tape

Follow these instructions:

1. From one end of each board, make a mark every 18".
2. Mark the center of the board at each 18" increment.
3. Drill 1" holes about 1/2" deep, then drill the rest of the hole with 3/8" bit.
4. Cut the rope into 4-ft lengths using electrical tape to keep the rope from fraying.
5. Feed the rope through the holes and tie a knot on the bottom side that will fit into the 1" hole.
6. Tie handles on the top side of the rope if desired. (Although it may be best not to, with players' arm lengths and height varying.)

The instructions listed above are for five players on each pair of boards. You could shorten the boards for four players per pair if needed. Set up a relay course where two groups of ten compete. Half of each group can "ski" down with the other half waiting on the other end to "ski" back. First group finished is the winner. Or one half of the group could "ski" down and back, then the other half repeat. Skiing is defined in this case as five group members with one foot on each board and the group lifting and moving each board forward separately in a right/left sequence. Feet must always be on the board. This is a great team building activity for coaxing players to step forward as a leader, and every team member has to carry their own weight for the team to be successful. It will be worth your time and investment building the skis.

Pipes - Buy some (8-10) pool noodles that have a small hollow opening that runs from end to end. Cut them into different length sections. Then using a box cutter, cut out small openings (usually 2-4 and large enough for a marble to drop through) along the length of each section. Vary the pattern of openings in each noodle and rotate the noodle as you cut the openings. Divide your squad into two teams. Each player gets one section, and the team forms a line. The object is for each team to hold their sections together and get a marble all the way to the end into a cup. Players must hold their section only, and their hands can't connect the sections. If the marble is dropped, they have to start over. This is a marvelous game and mirrors responsibilities (different sized noodles) in a game.

9. Making Practice a Success

Practice can be a source of great reward when you feel your team "got it." It can also be frustrating when things go wrong. What do we need to do to make it successful?

There are many factors involved with a winning practice. Remember, you set the tone with respect to what is expected and, ultimately, what is accomplished. Keeping the ingredients listed below in mind could help you evaluate effectiveness. It's almost impossible to check them all off your list, but here are a few to consider.

Well prepared/planned - Outline the activities for the day. If you're a details person, list everything. Get to the field early and lay out your grids to maximize time.

Engaging/challenging - The players may need to see something new to stay engaged, or a twist on an activity you've used before. Change the routine if necessary. Expose them to new challenges such as limiting touches, smaller grids, smaller goals and numbers down situations.

Clear expectations/positive environment - Set the tone at the beginning with regard to what you expect. That being said, you may have to remind them again. Players will be willing to do more in an environment where encouragement, specific praise, and reinforcement are present.

Progressions/decision making - Be ready to move the activity to the next level when it becomes too easy, or you want to see how players respond to adverse conditions. Allow players to solve the challenges of the activity. Do your best not to jump in at every breakdown. Create independent thinkers who can do the same in the game.

Passion/enthusiasm - If you bring it, your players have no choice but to jump in. Your passion will be contagious as long as it's genuine.

Competitive/rewarding - A great practice will leave players with a feeling of accomplishment knowing it will prepare them for that next game. Feed that competitive nature. Incorporate activities that allow players to compete against each other with a winner and a loser.

Flexible/adaptable - Recognize when an activity isn't working the way you planned and adjust it to maximize what you need to see, or create more success or pressure.

Paint successful pictures/encourage risks - When your players get it right, stop the action, praise, and recreate the picture for all to see. A positive mental picture will be a great asset for the game. Lift all restrictions in your last game. Give them the freedom to use their experience and skills to be creative.

Timely/relevant - Set up and plan practice with respect to what you saw as deficiencies or adjustments needed from your last game, and more importantly what your team needs to focus on for your next opponent.

Simulate match conditions/ encourage communication - When finding activities, find ones that have an element or elements that recreate game situations. If they don't, use your experience to make sure they do. Great teams are great communicators on the field. Emphasize and expect your players to communicate in every activity.

Feedback from players/assess players - When practice ends, allow your players time to give feedback on the day's activities. Everything you do should give you a view of players' current skill levels and areas that need work. Make sure to share that information with individual players.

Patience/realism - Some days, practice will be more of a challenge than others. Stay focused on the goal or goals you have for the day, and where your team is headed. If your team isn't performing to its potential, or the focus from the athletes isn't there, stop the activity and let them know. Should it be an individual player, take them aside and explain what you see. Remember, it's how you say it that will determine if your message has meaning.

* * *

Karen Vanover, former Athletic Director of the Year, and Coach at Lafayette High School in Lexington, KY shares her experience for making practice a success.

As an Athletic Director, I observed many practices for many sports at multiple levels. One constant factor for success was organization. The coach's degree of organization was evident to me within the first few minutes of observation.

An outline to follow for a new coach would start with the big picture (the whole season) and go through to minute detail (skills, tactics, strategies, etc.).

Big picture:

- Look at the whole season and see how many practices you will have. Are you a swimming coach and only get the pool three times a week, and have a 12-week season? You have 36 water practices. Can you do dry land practices on the days you don't have the pool? Figure that in as well.

- Next, outline the skills you need to teach/practice. Use a logical order to the skills and build in progressions that increase with conditioning and fitness. How much time will it take to master each skill? Can you add a similar skill without them mastering the first? Keep in mind that you need to introduce all the main skills before the first game or meet. List all the skills from easy to hard and put them in your practice calendar.

- Include game situations, scrimmages, and strategies in your season-long practice plan. After the game/meets start, you will know what areas you need to work on the most. Don't forget to have a session with the players about the rules. You might even have them read the rule book themselves so they can take ownership of the rules.

Daily practices:

- Your WRITTEN practice for every day should include warm up, skill set, drills, cool down and closure to the practice (what is working well, what needs work, what is coming up for the week). Not only will having a written plan (like a lesson plan for teaching) keep you on track to cover all the skills, you will have a paper trail if you are accused of negligence (leaving out necessary skills, rules, and conditioning) in the event of an injury to a player.

- Make a template that you can use for everyday practice broken down into time and activity and make copies. Then you can just write in the date and what you are doing that day.

- Keep notes after each practice to be sure you covered all the skill sets you'd planned for the day and make notes about what drills worked or didn't and why. Even though your daily plans will change every year (season flow will be determined by your players' skills), it will be a helpful outline for the next year.

- Leave room for the "teachable moment," a situation that comes up and should be addressed right then. This might occur with skills, but often time it works its way into areas like game strategy, team building, responsibility to the team, responsibility for their actions, decision making, etc. If you think of something your team needs to work on but can't get to it that day, you can make a note on your daily practice sheet and add it the next day.

Most of us admit that, by the end of the season, practice can be boring. You only have so many skill sets to work on. To keep practice fun, fresh and of value:

- Rotate drills. If one is not working, don't just keep making them do the same one over and over till they get it. Find a different way to help them master the skills you are looking for.

- Give your players a skill set and let them pick the drill to practice that skill.

- Know when practice is stale and not of any value. Some boredom-busters include playing a different sport (if you are practicing VB, play flag football instead for the day); have a parent bring ice cream or pizza at the end of practice; kidnap them and go to a fun place like a trampoline center, a local park, a pool, etc.

Being spontaneous can be a useful tool, but be sure to think through it. One of my coaches recognized boredom and surprised the team by calling off practice. However, he didn't tell the parents, the AD, or anyone else. The players were pretty much unsupervised for the two hours they were supposed to be practicing. One of the parents came to pick up her daughter for a doctor's appointment and none of us knew where they were. It was pretty embarrassing and could have been a legal issue.

Being organized is a skill every coach should master. With a little practice, it will become second nature.

* * *

Practice is the key to success in every game. It's our job to prepare the team to the best of our ability. That importance should never be taken for granted.

Every player loves the day they put that uniform on for your school. It's their time to shine for their team, their family, and themselves. As you watch them play, keep in mind that shine comes from their hard work and dedication in practice. And it's you who, through careful planning, provides the environment for them to become the players they are.

10. Can You Coach Any Player?

Think back over your career. How many different personalities have you coached? Which ones gave you the fewest problems? Which were the most challenging? If you could choose the quintessential athlete, what personality would they have? Is it important that their personality conforms to your standards or needs?

With so many personalities to deal with, it's imperative you have the ability to deal with (and relate to) an inner-city player, a suburban player, an introvert, extrovert, skeptic, or social butterfly. When you think about it, a coach's job is pretty unique.

We all have days when we go home and think, "That player is driving me crazy!" So, what are the traits you'd wish every player to have when they come to you? Perhaps you would like only to have a player who never questions your decisions, offers ideas when appropriate, never causes any problems, has a great work ethic, and is an inspiration to everyone else on the team. Wouldn't we all?! But, on second thoughts, would we?

Personalities are like skills… everyone is different, at different levels. Players don't all have the skill sets needed to play quarterback, goalkeeper, outfielder, point guard, or pitcher. Your team needs players suited for other positions as well. So why should we wish they were all packaged in a conforming, robotic persona to accommodate our coaching style?

Let's remember why we got into coaching. Certainly, it was our passion for the game, but it was also due to the test and invigoration of dealing with players who present challenges. Instead of focusing on the players, let's focus on the traits you need – as a coach – for dealing with all the unique players that come to you every day.

Be yourself - There's no need to become an inner-city coach when you have no real idea what it's like to grow up there. The same is true for any place. You have your very own special personality and relationship to unique life experiences. Use them to your advantage.

Relate - Much is made about being too old or too young to relate to players. There are many instances where a young or old coach took a team to the championship, or was a huge success in developing players. Being able to relate to players has nothing to do with age. It has everything to do with openness, intuition, integrity, and honesty.

Hall of Fame Swimming Coach Dave Barney shares what is essential in reaching your athletes. From his article, "The Magic of Motivation...or Not."

Despite the ironic ambiguity present in the title of this essay, there is no magic, there is no sleight of hand, no abracadabra, no hocus-pocus, no rabbits pulled out of hats even in this give and take between athlete and coach, merely style and a fundamental faith in the idea that trust and mutual respect and understanding determine the degree to which a coach reaches an athlete.

* * *

Listen - Let your players tell you everything about themselves, and the area they grew up in. Just by listening to their stories, you are relating in a way that very few before you have. Nothing brings a player more joy than reliving their journey from childhood to now. You only have to see their faces as the experiences come to life to realize how true that is.

Respect - Respect your players for who they are, not where they came from. Don't try to change or attack their personalities. If they have bad habits, work with them, but let the flavor of who they are shine through.

Communicate - Be clear in your expectations on and off the field. Paint a picture of how you expect them to conduct themselves. Highlight how personality is a plus in tough game situations, and that's one of the reasons they made your team.

* * *

Dave Barney also gives us valuable insight on motivation and the role of communication.

Motivation begins with the individual. Self-motivation, then, is a prerequisite to anything motivational that a coach might provide. Maybe it's best to keep in mind that motivation by itself is never ever a given, nor even some imaginary script that only a coach might know. I guess, in the long run, it could be considered a psychological calculus of sorts. Toward that understanding, then, the most important challenge for a coach resides in his or her role as a sports psychologist, since athletic performance is mainly mental. Any guy in a gorilla suit can train a swim team physically, mentally is another matter altogether. Within the frame of that thought reside all the mental challenges associated with motivation. Remember also that motivation begins with and balances upon a fulcrum called communication. Without the latter, there can be little hope of achieving the former.

* * *

Trust - Allow them room to grow. There's no need to jump in at every moment you sense change is needed. Trust them enough to see how they handle the situation, whether in a game or just a situation with a teammate.

Conviction - When you have to make a tough decision, do it with conviction. Some decisions aren't easy, but they have to be made. Nothing deteriorates your ability to lead a team more than delaying or avoiding decisions.

Consistency - Every team needs a leader, a rock. Consistency allows players to worry about one thing – playing. They need to know you'll handle the difficult decisions in a consistent and timely manner. Allow your players to play, and be their leader.

While it's nice to have some common ground for every player you recruit, or who plays for you, it isn't always necessary. Often our best friends are completely opposite personalities and come from other parts of the world. It isn't that we need to be like them, it's the fact that we complement each other, and find them interesting. So it is the same with coaching. There should never be any pressure to have a personal connection to a player's old neighborhood, school or area.

Let's remember, they came to us to play sport. That's what we need to focus on. If we stay true to our intuition, listen at every chance, model our integrity and lead with honesty and consistency, our ability to relate to our players will develop with respect and admiration.

Just let their personalities shine!

11. What Are Your Players Searching For?

Have you seen the "The Wizard of Oz"? If so, you're familiar with Dorothy, the Lion, the Scarecrow, and the Tin Man, all searching for something they already have. Dorothy wants to get back home to her family, the Lion wants courage, the Scarecrow wants a brain, and the Tin Man wants a heart.

Ironically, the great and powerful Oz, who has the power to help them, is only a common man behind a curtain.

For me, The Wizard of Oz is a great analogy for coaching. It asks the question: are we the person behind the curtain, convincing our players we have all the answers and they already have what they need to be successful?

Yes, coaching to a big degree is selling the truth, an idea, a concept, a vision, a dream. It's easy if you believe what you're selling and you do it in a genuine way with players' benefits first and foremost.

Believing and being confident are also attributes all successful players have. They know who they are and understand they have the ability to accomplish great things. They just need a coach to help them realize their own powers.

The Wizard gave Dorothy and her friends a difficult challenge to prove they deserved his favor (getting the broom of the Wicked Witch). How can you convince a player to believe in themselves? If they don't, it doesn't matter how much you believe in them. Without that belief, they won't be as successful as they should be.

You don't have to send them out to contend with scary monkeys and an evil witch, however. Instead, start with a one-on-one session with these questions and statements to guide the conversation:

- How do you see yourself individually and as part of the team?
- Specifically, what do you want to accomplish?
- Is playing basketball/baseball/football/etc. what you really want? Why?
- What do you believe will be the sacrifices needed to play?
- What strengths do you have that will get you through adversity?
- Why should teammates believe in you?
- Let them know their teammates are counting on them.

- What can you (as the coach) specifically do to help them?
- Reaffirm how much you want them to succeed.

You may want to share some of these touchpoints with your players before the meeting so they can put down some thoughts in preparation.

There are certainly times when a coach's vision of players is miles apart from what those players want to become, how they see themselves and, frankly, the level of effort they want to put forth to get there. They may be playing to please their parents or friends more than playing for their own benefits. As a coach, you need to know that. Spending time pushing someone where they don't want to go may be unproductive and fruitless.

In other cases, sitting down with the player and listening to their ideas of where they are now, and what they want to accomplish, gives you new insight on how best to guide this player. The key is to listen carefully. Even if you hear things you don't want to hear, or you think are irrelevant, there will be clues on how best to coach this player. Be patient by letting them speak. Often, when they're allowed to hear and formulate what they've said in a moment of silence, they understand how one thing may not be the best direction to take. Remember, there are no right and wrong comments in these meetings. Trust is built when they know they can speak openly and honestly.

It's okay for a player not to want to become the next superstar. There are other goals to accomplish in the game both for their sake and that of their teammates. Our mission is to find the best way to coach our players as individuals and blend them all together into a team.

There's no need for us to hide behind a curtain as if we are the all powerful Oz and know everything. Our objective should always be to use every resource possible to provide a positive, challenging, and caring environment within which our players will grow and improve. The key will be convincing them they already have what they're searching for. They just need someone to say it.

12. Fixer Upper

There's a big market now for shows on television that follow 'makeovers'. Shows such as *Fixer Upper*, *Flip or Flop*, and *Property Brothers*. The concept is based on taking a house that needs renovating, having a vision for what it could be, and taking the risk to invest the time and money required to turn it around.

I realized that what they do with houses is not so far removed from what we sometimes face: taking on a program with issues, having a vision, and providing a willingness to invest in the energy needed to rebuild it.

There are many houses (programs) with shrubs growing out of control hiding the house, terrible floor plans, and outdated floors and cabinets. Many potential owners (coaches) drive by those houses every day not willing to take on the challenge.

What if someone contacted you about a team that was dealing with the challenges listed below? Would you consider it? Would you recognize it as a program with good bones that only needs someone with skill to get renovating?

- History of losing season(s)
- Depleted roster
- Little to no community support
- Parent complaints
- Disruptive player(s)
- Terrible facilities
- No respect (officials, other coaches)
- Tough district/region
- Lost every playoff game
- Uninspired Administrator(s)
- No media support

I'm pretty sure you'd say there's no way you'd want to coach a team with so many problems. But is there another way to look at it? When you filter through all the obvious negatives, this team may just need a leader. This is a wonderful opportunity to put your stamp on a team that needs you more than any championship team. Will it take a lot of work and time? No doubt, but just about everything mentioned is fixable through dedication, commitment, and determination.

Certainly one of the reasons we coach is that we like challenges and, in that sense, this is a goldmine. It will take some time, but the satisfaction of building a successful team and program will be far greater than anything you could imagine.

What steps could you take to renovate the program?

Meet with Administrators - Sell them on your vision and how much you'll need their support to accomplish your goals. Share with them an immediate plan, a five-year plan, and a ten-year plan. Emphasize the broad benefits of a successful program to the school. They need to see you're more than a coach. You're a leader just like them.

Meet with the team - This may be your toughest meeting. They've seen others like you come and go, so they'll be skeptical. Remember, only your actions, dedication, and willingness to assist them every day will gain their trust. Work with them on establishing team expectations and accountability. Be consistent in every decision you make.

Meet with parents - Keep in mind they are hungry for a successful program that highlights their son's or daughter's ability. Let them know how much you need their help in building a first-class program. They should understand what you expect and what they can expect from you. Share the expectations you have for their son or daughter so there is no confusion.

Meet with your Athletic Director - Work on a new budget. Walk the field and facilities. Work with him or her to set a timeline for improvements, and areas that must be taken care of immediately. Also, develop a five-year-plan for everything you have in mind.

Contact local media - Go to their place of business if possible and thank them for their past support. Lay out guidelines for pre-season interviews, times to talk with players and coaches, etc. Build a solid relationship with reporters so they can count on you for a good story. Also, ask if there is anything you can do to make you or your team more accessible.

Walk your school - Meet every student and teacher you can during the day. Explain to teachers the expectations you have for your players' conduct when in class, and to contact you if they get out of line. Be passionate when talking with students, so they want to attend your games.

Visit your community - When time allows, visit local businesses and find out how your team can help with community projects or needs. Make sure they know they can count on you if needed. Let them know how much you appreciate their support.

One of my favorite parts of renovation shows is the ending when you see the smiles, tears, and joy of the new owners with what has been accomplished. I'm sure you've felt the same way when your team has been transformed throughout a season. It's a feeling that reminds you of why you coach.

There are teams that need our perseverance and leadership. Those are the ones we can make the most difference with, and impact players' lives in a positive way. It's not always about winning a championship; it's about building something when no one gave it a chance.

Get out your tools and draw your blueprint; it's time to build something special.

13. Shaping the Character of Your Team

Have you ever said, "That's not who we are!" or "We're better than that!"

How do you deal with, and mold, the character of your team? Adverse situations can and will happen, and they can be great learning experiences, but do your players understand self-discipline and know what you expect. You shape and mold their understanding of those expectations long before the season begins. Every day, in practice, you have the opportunity to model behavior and self-discipline. A veteran coach once told me, "Explain it to them a thousand times, and then explain it again."

Here are a few examples of an undisciplined team:

- In winning a game easily against a lesser opponent, attitudes turn to selfishness, self-serving actions, boasting, and laughter on the bench.

- While losing to an average opponent, players start bickering and blaming each other on the field, and act immaturely on the bench when removed from play.

- Constant berating of officials.

- Talking trash with opponents, leading to confrontations.

- Showing up fashionably late for practice and games.

- Throwing shoes or ripping off jerseys in disgust on the sidelines.

- Yelling at the coach.

Most of us have witnessed these types of incidents with other teams, and in some cases, our teams. I could go on and on with examples. But, the point is, have you taught your players how to conduct themselves when these situations occur? Have they been taught self-discipline?

Coaches often ask themselves and others, "What are they being taught at home?" Rather than blame parents, because we may not know the whole story, we have to teach them every day how to conduct themselves appropriately while they're on our team.

It really bothers me when a winning team starts laughing and yelling during a blowout game and players become selfish, begging to play up front to score a goal. It's equally as bad when you're on the losing end of the scoreboard and players start yelling at each other as the game goes on. Suddenly, true character exposes itself in an adverse situation. It's certainly bothersome to me as a coach.

What steps can you take to shape the character of your team?

- Establish clear expectations with the team that are non-negotiable.
- Remind the team of these expectations every day and explain them to the parents before the season.
- Set the tone and be firm and consistent when accountability is necessary.
- Be a model of the behavior you expect from your players every day.
- Applaud and highlight outstanding behavior, especially in adverse situations.
- Deal with an incident, in a professional way, the moment it happens.
- Follow up the next day with a meeting with the player or players.
- Remember that accountability is the same regardless of status.
- Never waiver in your responsibility as a coach.

Often coaches will let a team vote on disciplining a player. This can be a slippery slope. More often than not, teammates will vote to let the player play if it's a big game or some other event. My experience is most teams just want their teammate back in, and don't want to deal with the negative feelings should they vote for them to be disciplined. Coaches know this, and it gives them an out because the team voted a player back in and allows the player to play. Just go ahead and do what's right and take care of the accountability yourself. Your credibility is on the line because players know this is your job, not theirs.

There will be times and situations where a player acts out of character in a negative way. Often the reason has to do more with something away from the field than on it. There also will be times when a player has no excuse for their actions. In each case, it's important for you to maintain your composure and discipline the player accordingly. Once you start bending the rules, you've opened the door for the next incident because all the players are watching.

Your team will always be a reflection of what you expect. Set the standard high and be consistent in what you will allow. Your players may not say thank you, but they will be proud to be part of a program that clearly defines who they are, and what they can become.

14. Team Chemistry... What is it?

Have you had a team that exemplified Team Chemistry? What exactly is it? What led you to believe your team had it? That phrase is often thrown around in conversations, about a team that's successful, but is it a necessity for success? Do all your players have to like each other? Let's look at some characteristics of teams that work together well:

Five building blocks of team chemistry

1. **Responsibility** - Players won't always be friends or hang out with their teammates away from the game. That's okay. You can't make someone like someone else. It is, however, their responsibility to realize how much they need their teammates (and how much their teammates need them) during practice and in the game to be successful.

2. **Tolerance** - Often teammates won't have the same values, or come from the same culture that others were exposed to. It's important for them to see that people might not always agree, but they can leave those differences outside the lines during the game. On game night, we all wear the same jersey.

3. **Role clarity** - As a coach, defining your players' roles may be your most important job. Never assume players know what you expect, or how you see them contributing to the team. Have an individual meeting with each player and share your thoughts. Encourage the player to share their vision. It may be a role you never envisioned.

4. **Deference** - Players who carry the load, and receive recognition in the media have the opportunity to create or destroy more team chemistry than any other player. If they show humility and mention their teammates at every opportunity, the team is well on its way to achieving positive Team Chemistry.

5. **Technical skill** - Teammates can assist each other through an understanding of each other's responsibilities. When a player threads a perfect pass, or times a run with precision, that is often referred to as Team Chemistry. Highly skilled players have to recognize when to adjust and not become frustrated by players with lesser abilities.

I've had teams that were successful despite their dislike for each other outside the game. When they stepped across the line to begin the game, they fought relentlessly for each other. When the game was over, their dislike resurfaced just as quickly as it disappeared. Keep in mind that Team Chemistry on the field may often have little to do with how players *interact* off the field. As a coach, be concerned with what you can control, and know that players are under no obligation to like each other. If it carries over to the field, or gets out of control, that's when you have to step in. At that point, it can't be tolerated. I recommend bringing in the parties involved, listening to their sides of the story, and then giving them a choice of working it out or saying you will make the appropriate decisions for the betterment of the team.

Let's take a look at some ideas that can bring your team together. It takes a lot of work for a player not to understand, not be tolerant, or not to accept another player after experiencing the following seven 'team builders' together:

Shaping team chemistry

1. **Team leadership** - It starts with the coach. Create a vision and a plan of action to lead your team. Players who are team leaders are a must! Put them in charge of team building activities/projects, creating expectations and making the new players feel welcome. A Leadership Council composed of six veteran players is a great idea to deal with challenges and issues the team faces.

2. **Team building** - Team Chemistry is most often developed away from the field, as players get to see themselves and others in a different light. Research team building activities appropriate for your team.

3. **Community projects** - Have players volunteer at a homeless shelter serving food, have them visit a nursing home or a halfway house. Maybe even get them to go to a hospital for young children. The benefits they receive from this project will easily bond them together, and their impressions will last a lifetime.

4. **Big sister/little sister** - Match your veterans with the incoming freshmen. Have them exchange token gifts or cards on a couple of occasions, and spend time getting to know each other. The younger player should feel comfortable asking the veteran about challenges with the team.

5. **Secret pal** - Have team members draw someone else's name and keep the names secret. At various times, have them give each other cards, token gifts, words of praise, etc. They can secretly give the coach the gift to pass on, as a go-between, to remain anonymous.

6. **Overnight trips** - Traveling to camp or a weekend of games really brings a team together. While on the road, players are free to spend time together and talk about areas of their lives that don't pertain to soccer.

7. **Fun outing** - Take your team to an amusement park, bowling alley, waterpark, or other venue to get them away from the game. It allows them to relax and have fun together without the pressure that comes with the game.

Team Chemistry is a living, breathing part of your team. There will be days when you see none of it and players are frustrated. But there will be times when everything is going right on and off the field, and Team Chemistry is blooming. As a coach, you can create an atmosphere where players are encouraged to bond and come together to benefit the team. That environment will ultimately play a huge part in how successful your team is.

When you create a program based on every player knowing and understanding their roles, you'll have a team that will work harder than ever before for their teammates. Take the time to build the chemistry.

My definition of Team Chemistry:

A team that understands the responsibility they have to each other to perform to their very best at practice and a game. A team that is tolerant, defers success to their teammates, and which understands how important everyone's role is on the team while rejoicing in teammates' success.

15. Captains... What do you expect?

"Coach, I need your captains." A phrase I've heard hundreds of times from officials as game time draws near.

How do you select captains for your team? I must admit, captain has never been a word I've warmed to. My mind flashes to someone who thinks they're better than everyone else, someone who wants all the glamour and says, "Look at me!"

What exactly are you looking for in a captain? Here are some characteristics to consider as you formulate your own list.

- Humble
- Communicator
- Competitive
- Encourager
- Strong work ethic
- Composed
- Confident
- Willing to confront
- Mentally tough
- Trustworthy

A quote I've shared with several of my teams while choosing captains still rings true:

"Captains aren't necessarily Leaders, and Leaders aren't necessarily captains. We need Leaders. Captains have status, Leaders have courage."

To me, that says it all. I want Leaders on and off the field. They're the ones who never take a day off, encourage others, and even get in the face of teammates not doing their jobs. Leaders have to live on the edge, knowing when to challenge their teammates and when to back off. They're willing to risk friendships for the benefit of the team. If you have one or more, consider yourself blessed. I've found at the high school level they can be rare. It's a huge challenge to transform a player who lacks courage into a true leader.

The majority of my teams have always wanted captains, and I've always shown my reluctance to name or select them for the whole season. There are various ways to select them: Team-chosen, Coach-chosen, or a combination of Team and Coach. Along with that, many coaches set the criteria for those being nominated, with respect to academic grades, conduct, achievements, character, etc.

There are traps with each selection process. If the team votes, it could be based on friendship (even the opposite!), or someone the coach really objects to. If the coach selects, it could be perceived by the team as a pet player, and you take away accountability and responsibility from the team for not trusting them to select. If coaches and players select, neither side may feel good about the process, having to live with someone they wouldn't have chosen.

* * *

Athletic Director and former coach, Karen Vanover, highlights some of the challenges involved when selecting captains.

One choice coaches have to make is whether to have team captains or not. Not all sports need a captain for games and some coaches consider themselves "The Captain." Teams that have very small numbers, such as golf and cross country, for example, may not really need one.

Ask yourself what role your captains will play – does the game require it for the coin toss and/or for rule briefing at the beginning of the game? Are your captains players who can bring the team together and get them focused? Is the captain a liaison between the coaches and players? Are they fully invested in the team and school? What do you expect from them?

Another big question is how will you decide on captains? Are seniors automatically captains? Do you decide? Does the team vote? How many will you have?

The bottom line is that once you start selecting captains one way it may be a challenge to change the process from one season to the next. How they are chosen should be based on their character, leadership skills, solid work ethic, and being respected by their teammates. They should know your expectations and consult with you whenever in doubt.

Captains can be a great asset for the team but they can also create issues when there are none, without your guidance and expectations.

Have you ever considered conducting screening interviews for potential captains? They could be required to fill out an application with an introductory letter. During the interview which could include some members of the team and a coach from another sport, or administrator, here's a list of potential questions:

- Why do you want to be a captain?

- What responsibilities do you see yourself carrying out? Which ones are most important to you?

- Why should teammates listen to you?

- What traits do you have that will make you a good leader?

- How will you react when a teammate attacks your effort and attitude?

- What would you say to a teammate whose attitude disrupts the team?

- How will you work with teammates that can't get along?

- Describe a situation where being passionately reactive would be necessary?

- What would you say to a teammate that's thinking of quitting?

- Are you a vocal leader or leader by example?

- How will you respond when you disagree with a specific decision by the coach?

- What situation or challenge bothers you the most?

* * *

Molly Grisham, Owner, Influencer, and Lead Facilitator at Influence LLC lends her valuable experience of working with teams as a coach and consultant to help us recognize the skills necessary to be a captain.

I often hear from coaches who are frustrated because their players see the selection of team captains as a popularity contest, an award presented to a player for time dedicated to the team, an honor for the best player, or a role held for exclusively for seniors. I disagree with those perspectives.

I believe team captains need specific skills to lead a team. The selection of team captains should include an assessment of a player's leadership skill set. Being a team captain is an additional job and this job requires skills to be effective. Too many coaches put the success of the team in the hands of appointed captains who do not have the skills needed to lead. Captains without the skills to lead are playing a role rather than doing a job.

Each coach can determine what skills they desire their team captains to possess. A few things that were important to me are: the communication skills to speak with me about what is going on with the team behind closed doors, the confidence to address teammates when issues arise, and the self-discipline to model a high standard of behavior.

In addition to having the skills needed to lead a team, captains should also have the desire to take the job. Some players just want to focus on playing and the additional responsibility of leading is seen as a burden in their eyes. I believe that coaches need to be clear in defining the job they are asking a player to accept. Ultimately a player can decide if they are interested in taking the job.

When we see being a team captain as a job with a necessary skill set, we then help our players to hire the most qualified candidates.

* * *

My question is, "How urgent is it that you have yearlong captains, especially if they aren't your Leaders?"

An option to consider is naming "captains for the night," based on their last performance or simply rotating it among seniors or upperclassmen as required. At the high school level, players enjoy the status symbol of being captain for a night. Going up for the coin toss, being the one the referee seeks out during the game, and being able to have their friends see them in this role is rewarding to them. It has very little to do with leadership and that's why I do it this way. Are there nights when my Leaders end up being my captains? Absolutely, but they're going to lead regardless of whether they're the captain or not. Leaders never hide.

In the early years, there was a time or two when I selected yearlong captains based on grade level expecting experience and maturity to be the key. That was a mistake. There is no such thing as a rite of passage to being a captain just because you're a senior. On every team, respect is earned on and off the field, not by grade.

Leaders are easy to spot on a team. They arrive at practice and the game before everyone else. They stay late. They grind it out every day whether they feel 100% or not. They lead by example and are usually vocal as well. Everything they do is for and about the team. They'll hug their teammates on a great play and yell at them when they know it could have been done better. They'll even be brave enough to question the coach, and may or may not be your best player. Status is never something they seek out.

Relish and appreciate every Leader you have, because you'll realize how important they were to your team when they're gone. Leaders, not captains, are what you and your team need. Just find the right way to allow them to be effective.

16. Considering Team Camp?

As summer begins, I feel certain that many of you will take your high school teams to a team camp at a university of your choosing. This was always a goal of our team. The benefits of attending a camp are valuable and always prove to be a rewarding experience. With that in mind, what do you look for when all the brochures and emails come pouring into your office during the winter? How do you decide where to attend? What are your goals for camp?

Here are some considerations:

1. Commute to a local university or travel away from home?
2. What coaching staff can effectively best assist my team?
3. Is the cost in line with the value and benefits?
4. What dates work best for my team?
5. What do I want my team to accomplish at camp?

While staying close to home may be attractive from a cost standpoint, the benefits of traveling and getting away from home are always the best. Having your team spend the entire week at camp gives you and them a new perspective. It allows you to keep distractions to a minimum and gives you the opportunity to observe your team. Plus, during downtime in the afternoons, you can meet with the team for team-building activities, goal setting, or just to relax and talk.

Strongly consider the strength and reputation of the coaching staff conducting the camp. Is their goal to assist your team in improving their skills? Are they able to highlight individuals' strong points, as well as making recommendations for improvement? If so, they deserve the opportunity.

Camp is a costly venture for some families, especially if each player is picking up the cost. If you've never attended a certain university's camp, ask for a detailed outline for each day and decide if it can benefit your team.

It may be impossible to attend the camp you would most like because the date or dates aren't compatible with your players' schedules for the summer. If that should happen, you may want to bring college staff to your field for a week and work with them there. Most college coaches are very agreeable. The downside, however, is that it doesn't allow you to play against other teams, but it is a great camp for individual attention, and your team is the only one the clinician is focused on.

What should I ask for from the Camp Director?

1. Qualified instructor, preferably a college coach.

2. Specific areas of instruction for my team.

3. Detailed practice plans from all the sessions, even the ones my team didn't participate in.

4. To be included in meetings concerning progress of the camp.

5. Safety and adult supervision in the residence hall at night.

First and foremost, be adamant about who will work with your team. As a coach, you want your team under the guidance of the best coach on the staff, someone who is knowledgeable, passionate, and will challenge the players. Recent college players who just graduated may not have the experience and leadership you need. Some are aspiring coaches, but your team doesn't need a friend – they need a coach. Who your team's instructor is, and how well they do their job, will determine if this camp is successful or not.

Before you get to camp, meet with your assistants and determine the areas that the team needs to focus on at camp. Is it passing, defending, maintaining possession, shape, finishing, support, getting forward, pressure, etc. Relay this information to the director and the coach who will work with your team.

Use camp to pick up new ideas and concepts. It's easy to get the ones from the coach working with your team – you'll be with them every day. What about the ones from the other teams' instructors? Ask the director to make sure all the camp coaches make their plans available to you and the other coaches. They're great resources from coaches with years of experience you can take advantage of.

Ask to be included in all meetings pertaining to the progress of camp and plans for each day. Remember, for the most part these meetings are for the staff, so respect what they say, and only intervene when asked.

Safety has to be your number one concern when attending a residential camp. Be familiar with who is supervising your players, and go over the rules and expectations with your team so there are no misunderstandings. Make sure every player has your cell phone number in case of emergency.

Great activities that some camps offer

(Obviously, activities will vary depending on the sport, but here are two that work well for soccer.)

4 v 4 Dutch tournament - A great activity for getting players together on the first day of camp. You can research it, but here are the particulars.

Players rotate to a new team after each game. They get 10 points for a win and 1 point for every goal their team scores. 5 points for a draw and 0 points for a loss. Teams that lose still count their goals.

Setup and Rules:

1. Field size is 30 X 20 yds.
2. Goals are a pair of cones each end.
3. 6 or 8-minute games.
4. Ball must be on the ground when it passes through goal.
5. A ball that goes out of bounds is kicked in from the point it went out.
6. No keepers, players ref their own games.

The advantages are:

1. 4 v 4 allows more touches.
2. Playing with different players each game, so they have to communicate and adapt.
3. Players ref their own games so they have to sort out their own problems.
4. One team won't dominate.
5. Individual players will be taken out of their comfort zone which is good for development.

7 v 7 World Cup Extravaganza - One of the best nights of any camp I've ever attended. Each team is given a World Cup Team at the beginning of camp. At some point, their coach or someone from the team goes to a store and picks up face paint, flags, t-shirts, etc. for the team. That night, all the teams file into the stadium like the Olympics, and play a round robin 7 v 7 tournament into the night. Being from Norway, our camp director dressed like a Viking to lead the teams in. It was awesome!

A trip to a Water Park - Time permitting, a relaxing time for teams on an afternoon when the heat index is too high to practice outside.

Talent Show - Each team has to come up with a skit for talent night! I'm always amazed at how talented our players are with respect to other aspects of their lives. Coaches can be on the judging panel. It can even be conducted like "America's Got Talent".

Perform a song - Each team or group selects a song from their phone, practices the lyrics, and performs it in any form they choose (words must be appropriate and performers should use discretion). Give each team 10 minutes to prepare. If possible, have the coach or coaches do their own version as a sample. This can be conducted during a separate team building session during the day.

Team Building - Take some ideas and material to camp with you, in case you have time to do some team building of your own with your team.

The key to camp will always be your passion and enthusiasm for everything the players are doing. There will be days when the players are tired and irritable, and they'll need your encouragement to help them continue. Every chance you get, be involved in all the team building and fun events. Your willingness to show another side of yourself will allow your players to relax and realize the enjoyment of being there. Camps are always a memory of a lifetime. Players will remember special moments and special events (which they did, or you did) when at camp. The togetherness and bonding that comes from being there is priceless and will benefit you and your team in ways you never imagined.

17. How Can You Maintain Success?

Have you considered what you'll do when your team experiences success? We all see our teams being successful, at some point, but are we ready for it? What if you have a season when everything falls into place and success comes pouring out like water from a faucet? Will you know what made the difference? Was it your great job of coaching? Was it your players? Was the competition less challenging than in other years?

I think we'd agree there are several factors that contribute to your success. Probably the first one you might (selfishly) think of is your coaching ability. Upon experiencing success, you may tell yourself, "This is easy, I've got this figured out," or "My system is superior to those for the other teams." Quite frankly, it's easy to fall into this trap; everyone around you tells you how good you are, and your ego inflates! Ironically, it's the same trap you warn your players about when they experience success.

What about a season when nothing seems to work? Just when you think you've become a great coach, it's as though you invented a new formula for things going wrong!

You may be an outstanding coach, but you have to keep your hunger and passion, evaluating each season and continuing to work diligently to maintain a high standard of success.

How can we keep our teams playing at the highest level, year after year?

1. Review last year's practice schedule. Strengths and Weaknesses.

2. Write down five things that you feel contributed to last year's success or lack of success.

3. What were last year's team goals? Did we accomplish them? Were they challenging?

4. What were last year's individual goals? Were they accomplished? Were they challenging?

5. Was last year's game schedule tough enough? This season's schedule?

6. Have five people, (you, AD, parent, Assistant Coach, and player), evaluate your performance from last season. Focus on commonalities.

7. Were players positioned properly? Were there areas of concern?

8. Is it time to change the routine? Are the players bored and unengaged?

9. Did you make the best use of your assistant coaches?

10. Make a list of what you can control and what you can't. Throw the ones you can't control away.

11. Were your players involved in the decision-making process?

12. Were there any tough decisions you failed to make last season?

13. Look in the mirror and ask, "Am I 100% committed to coaching this team?"

14. Were you flexible early in the year with respect to trying players in different positions, and building for the post-season, or were you only concerned with winning individual games?

15. Did you listen to your players?

16. Did you adapt your system to your players or did they have to fit your system?

17. Did you include team building in your pre-season?

18. Did you take time to do something special for the team?

19. Were leaders established for the team? Were they effective?

20. Was there anything you would have changed or done differently?

What about involving others in the evaluation process? Who best knows what the team went through and whether it worked or not? Your players. Are you willing to seek their input and observations? Some you may not agree with, but they may cause you to pause and rethink certain situations. What questions should we ask? Here are a few to consider.

1. Would you consider our season a success? Why or why not?

2. If you could change anything about the season, what would it be?

3. How would you describe our practices?

4. How would you rate the team leadership of our program from 1-10?

5. What are two areas you would change with how we approach a game?

6. If you rated our team with respect to technical, tactical, psychological and physical, which is strongest? Weakest?

7. What is one area of our coaching that could be strengthened?

8. How would you rate the team's "mental toughness"?

9. List one specific thing that will help us reach our goals.

10. What are your thoughts as we look forward to next season?

Asking yourself tough questions at the end of the season will strengthen your ability to lead the team. I've had coaches tell me they took winning and success for granted, and didn't realize it until their teams started losing and new challenges surfaced. It's certainly easy to do. There aren't any guarantees, but by having a list of priorities you visit every year, you're taking steps to keep your team in position to achieve their goals.

18. Coaching a Gifted Player

Will you recognize a truly gifted player who, by the time they're a junior or senior, you will have little left to contribute towards? Someone who outgrows what you can offer in terms of skill and knowledge development. It can happen at any level, regardless of your background as a player or coach, and it can be a little unsettling.

If your extraordinary athlete has a great attitude and work ethic, with the goal of playing at the next level, their development path is a joy. They literally become a coach on the field, or floor, in practice and the game. However, if they use the situation in a negative way – slacking off, playing as an individual, and thinking they know it all – it can turn into a nightmare.

Remember, you have the control that affirms and encourages a positive work ethic; the control that can alter a less-than-desirable path of underutilized talent and opportunity. Contribute in both situations.

* * *

Hall of Fame Swimming Coach Dave Barney who has led Albuquerque Academy to 38 State Championships explains what coaches can do to assist great players. From his article, "The Magic of Motivation…or Not."

Now, most of us coaches are not trained psychologists, but somewhere in the reign of years, in the sphere of our experience, in our day-to-day contact with our athletes, we somehow gain a sense of what perhaps may inspire them to wave goodbye to images in the rear-view mirror of what they have already accomplished and look ahead, down the road a piece to a sign-post pointing the way toward possibility, a landscape, no matter the perils, that at one moment in their competitive lives they might have thought impossible to reach. When our swimmers go there, do that, they are moved mostly by their own convictions, their own strength of heart, their own collective will powers, and not by coaches cracking a whip. Whenever and however a coach embraces those moments, he or she should stress the positives, eliminate the negatives, abandon any thoughts about limitations. In other words, be an encourager of the highest order. Draw upon what many of us have come to know as "scratching the itch," namely the thought that reward is usually accompanied by risk or more precisely, perhaps, the willingness to take high school races out like "gangbusters." as I'm fond of saying. Challenge athletes to adopt this mantra, this "scratching the itch," mentality, if you will.

* * *

You would think that finding a truly gifted athlete who exceeds your ability to coach would not happen very often. After all, we're the coaches, and we have the knowledge and experience to assist every player. However, if you've coached that same gifted player since they were in the sixth grade, or as a club player who started with you as a U10, by the time they're a senior or a U17 player, they've seen every practice activity in your files many times! So now what will you do? At this point in their career, how will you keep them engaged and make practice and development a positive/learning experience for the player?

Here are a few tips to engage gifted players and your team:

Academics - Stress how important grades are to your player. If they want to stay eligible to play for you, and move on to the next level, academic standings are a must. Focus on their classes and conduct.

Challenge - Continue to present challenging situations in practice. Players want new barriers to overcome every day. Challenge them mentally by asking questions, as well as situationally. It's what they live for.

Variety - Use various activities in practice to keep their minds fresh. Stay away from lines. Small-sided games where all players get maximum touches and have to make lots of decisions are best.

Guest Speaker - Bring a current or former high-level college player in to talk with your team about what it takes to play at the next level; detail what practice involves and the time requirements both in season and out. Gifted players, along with the rest of your team, need to hear this to motivate them.

Competition - Everything in practice needs to be scored with a winner and loser. Great players want to beat someone every time they play. A few burpees or pushups for the losing team and rewards for the winning team.

1 v 1's or 1 v 2's - Numbers even or numbers down. Can you succeed? Want to know how good a player is? Give the advantage to the other player (or players) and see who wins. They love this setup.

Individual Plan - Develop an individual workout plan for the player. They may need more than you can offer in practice. If that's the case, work with the player to develop their own workout they can do on their time.

Individual Skills Coach - Have another coach come in and work with the player, preferably outside regular practice time. A fresh new face with a different approach and new ideas can be a great way to keep things moving forward.

Communicate - Never stop communicating with the player. Stay close and develop a mentor relationship. Help them see what's possible with their ability.

Humility - Make certain your player knows how much they need their teammates. Great players can be a disruption or a blessing. Never let them get their head in the clouds and forget their teammates.

Next Level - Guide the player and family in choices and decisions. Your knowledge of working with players headed to the next level will be a great asset. Use it to develop and maintain a bond with the player and their family.

Community Project - Have players work with younger kids or those who are less fortunate. It's a great way for them to use their talent in a positive way and will help them see the bigger picture.

Consistent - Treat gifted players in the same way as you treat any player on your team. When you highlight them in conversations with your team, you're creating issues. If you mollycoddle them, they will lose all respect for you. Handling the pressure can be overwhelming, so let them know you're in control, and that they just need to relax and play; then all the pressure is on you.

She was a truly gifted player (let's call her Grace). At practice, Grace could strike a ball better than any player we had ever had, and her knowledge of the game at that age was unheard of. She was an eighth grader and a natural. As I shook hands with the private school's coach before the Varsity game, he commented, "Wow! Our Varsity players who watched the JV game were amazed at your player's ability. They were asking why she wasn't playing Varsity, and I reminded them that she was probably only an eighth grader." He was right, and yes, we were all impressed. I could hardly wait until next year when Grace would be in high school and could move up to Varsity.

Later in the year, we were runners-up to a perennial private school power in a very prestigious JV tournament. We thought it was a glimpse of our future. But, after that, things just fell apart.

In the high school setting, the following year, Grace needed help in the classroom, and the support just wasn't there. Freshman year in high school is always tough. New teachers, new schedule, new expectations and often different rules can be overwhelming to some students. As her academics suffered, Grace wasn't allowed to play. When she lost soccer, she lost interest in school and a vicious cycle emerged. We made every effort we felt was possible, but to no avail. Grace wouldn't be able to play for us.

It was as if we had caught a glimpse of a bright meteor streaking across the sky with brilliant colors. Sadly it disappeared all too quickly, but we were blessed to have seen it. It wasn't the storybook ending we had all hoped for, but situations beyond your control can often determine results. In situations like this, coaches always feel like they could have done more, and I'm no different. I was not as concerned about Grace's soccer and place on the team, but for helping her make it through school.

Throughout history, there have been prodigies, like Mozart, who dazzled and amazed the rest of the world with their abilities. At first, I feel certain, their teachers felt threatened by a child with so much talent.

Our job will always be to assist our players to become the best players they can be on the field or court. It is also our job to help them succeed in the classroom. At times, those players may need more than we can give through our normal techniques. Recognizing such situations and developing a plan to aid and challenge them should be a priority; it will be a rewarding experience as we watch them grow. Having our coaching abilities threatened by a prodigy should never enter our minds; after all, when they surpass what we can offer, we've done our job!

19. MVPs and All-Tournament

I've often wondered why we stress the word "team" to our youngsters so much when we single them out by naming MVPs, and All-Tournament players. Especially when they all contributed to a successful tournament or post-season.

Whether it's team sports such as soccer, baseball, football, basketball, or hockey, or some individual sports like tennis or swimming – outstanding players need support from teammates to showcase their talent.

In soccer, without a defender or goalkeeper winning the ball at the back, our striker wouldn't have scored. Without the possession maintained by our midfielders, we wouldn't have been able to run out the clock. The list of examples is endless, yet we still continue to highlight individual players at the wrong time.

I'm not totally against MVPs and All-Tournament players. There's a place and time to recognize their achievements. Just not at the end of a tough game when every player busted their behind giving all they had. In that scenario, everyone on our team should be the MVP, everyone on our team should be All-Tournament.

We played in a tournament a few years back, didn't make it to the finals, and I felt we didn't give our best effort collectively. The tournament director came to me as I was leaving and asked what two players I was nominating from the opposition, as well as our team, for All-Tournament. After pausing for a moment, I said, "We don't deserve anyone, give those to another team that's more deserving." By picking two players, I would have only justified and rewarded poor performance.

All-Tournament Players can be an issue, but none like those experienced by naming an MVP. Let me say that the majority of teams have an MVP, and all the players, coaches, parents and fans know who it is. It only becomes a challenge when *you* recognize it, especially at the wrong time. Let me say that again; it only becomes a challenge when *you* recognize it, especially at the wrong time. When you publicly name an MVP, it has the potential to create animosity, jealousy, and dissension within the team, affecting the ability to play together effectively in the next game or next season. In my experience, a team often hears only one thing: "The coach likes him/her more than me."

As a first-year coach, I was eager for the end of season banquet, in order to recognize our many achievements and hand out awards to the players. We had a player who was skillfully, and statistically, without a doubt our

MVP. The banquet went well, and I named her MVP. I had no idea the issues I had created. The next season, the players socially alienated this player, and when I confronted them, they said, "Ask her, she's your MVP."

In an effort to improve the individual awards selection process, some coaches set up a system where opposing coaches or a committee votes for the players, removing a bias the coach may have for their own team. This allows coaches to explain to dissenters that other coaches or a committee voted and they couldn't vote for their own team. In other scenarios, coaches refuse to name All-Tournament Teams at lower level playoffs (such as District or Regional Tournaments) for fear of how it might affect the chemistry of the team should they move on. Their recommendation is to name those players at the banquet.

There can be other issues as well, such as parents questioning why their son or daughter who happens to be a senior isn't named All-Tournament. Your philosophy on this potential issue might be worth mentioning at your first parent meeting. Parents need to know that All-Tournament awards are based solely on that tournament and nothing else, while State and National Awards, as well as being selected for All-Star games, are a reward for a great individual season.

Here's a list to consider sharing with players and parents:

Individual awards

1. They are an honor and reflect your hard work. Remember your humility.
2. Will not win you a scholarship.
3. Never based on grade level.
4. Never give you elite status.
5. Voted on by a committee or coaches involved in the tournament.
6. Thank your teammates. Without them, it wouldn't have been possible.
7. We will never name an MVP. No one player is more valuable than another.
8. For performance in a particular game or games. Not for the season.
9. We will recognize these awards at the banquet.
10. All-State and All-Star game awards are voted on by all the state coaches.

Early playoff games against weak opponents, as well as a weak district or region, may present problems with respect to All-Tournament. As an example, your goalkeeper might be your best player, but only handles one or two balls during a two-game series. There is simply no way he or she is All-Tournament. All-Tournament is a wonderful opportunity, if they played well, to nominate a player that hasn't received much recognition throughout the year.

Should you name an MVP or All-Tournament player? Certainly, that's a decision you have to make in the best interest of your team with respect to maturity levels and dynamics. The fundamental question you have to ask is, "How important is it?"

I do believe strongly that you should reward outstanding performance by individuals every chance you get. Those players are the ones who will ultimately carry your team and are committed to success, and they deserve it. The key is when and how you do it.

20. Great Players

Can you control and bring a team together where one player dominates the landscape?

Having a player who tries to do everything – all the time – can be frustrating for the team, the player, and the coach. They become physically and mentally exhausted from working so hard, and ultimately become ineffective in the game. Their teammates start to watch this player rather than doing their own jobs on the field or court, and can feel inferior and resentful. But is this an example of a truly great player? What sets a great player apart from the player just referenced?

Great players realize it's a team game, and everyone must contribute and work together for the team to succeed. They're able to see key situations and moments throughout the game that others don't, requiring them to use their superior skills in a positive way to affect the outcome. They have a mental toughness and willingness to step up and carry the load, demanding the ball with the game on the line. Great players understand that to succeed, sometimes you must fail to gain valuable experience.

It's as though they're a superhero putting on their cape, or costume, and accomplishing unbelievable things to save the team. You can see it in their demeanor when situations arise:

Down 3-0 at the half! "We're better than this!"

We were trailing 3-0 at the half. I explained in firm tones that we weren't playing to our ability. As the players headed back on the field, I took one of our seniors, who I considered a great player, aside and said, "Nicole, we're better than this."

At the time she was our "go-to player," someone all the other players looked up to, and was willing to do anything possible to carry us to victory. I knew the message would resonate with her.

As the second half played down, we scored one, then two goals to tighten things up. You could see the confidence building with our players as they started encouraging each other. Two minutes were left, and we still trailed. We just couldn't get one in the back of the net, and I had almost come to the realization that we wouldn't win, but felt proud of how we fought back in this half.

Suddenly with 30 seconds left, Nicole won the ball at the top of the 18, and headed toward their goal. She was amazing, beating one of their strikers and two midfielders, and powering across the halfway line toward the goal.

The opposition that day had two very skilled defenders that weren't about to let her score, and they angled her away from the goal. At that moment, most people thought we were done, but not Nicole. She headed straight for the endline and, looking back, saw one of her teammates racing unmarked into the penalty box.

As Nicole got to the endline, she played a perfect back angle ball on the ground, across and away from the 6-yard box and the goalkeeper, to her teammate who simply ran onto the ball and placed it in the corner of the goal as the horn sounded. I'll never forget the celebration and what we had accomplished. Coming back from a three-goal deficit is almost unheard of in our game. We went on to win the game in a shootout.

Nicole would continue to be a great player throughout her career with us and have an outstanding college career.

* * *

Cy Tucker, 7-time Kentucky High School Girls Soccer State Championship Head Coach at South Oldham High School, shares the huge influence and responsibility great players bring to your team.

We were fortunate to have a lot of great players come through my program at South Oldham High School. We had many All-State selections and five high school All-Americans. There was one unique situation that occurred with one of them in 2013.

She was in the middle of her junior year season when I got word that my best player was talking to impressionable younger players about how high school soccer wasn't important and that she was considering quitting and just playing club year round.

This was a concern because she was a great player and was influencing younger players who looked up to her. My players had always expressed that they enjoyed high school soccer more than club.

During a JV game, I pulled her aside and confronted her with what I had heard. She didn't deny it. I then explained that I understood and appreciated the role of club soccer and that college coaches held club soccer in high regard. My comments included the fact that in club you are surrounded by teammates of the same age and similar abilities. In this environment, a player can showcase their skills to college coaches.

The conversation then shifted to the virtues of playing high school soccer. The most important one to me was that it showcases a player's character. When you have to compete with teammates of different ages and talent levels, it provides an opportunity to highlight your character. You become more tolerant. You find yourself being more supportive. You become a valuable role model. You elevate the play of those around you.

I wrapped up our conversation by saying that any college coach worthy of recruiting her should be looking for strength of character as well as playing ability.

She played well that day in a close loss to a local powerhouse team. The club talk stopped and she began to emerge as a leader on the team.

My point is that even your great players may need a little guidance as to what's best for them and the team.

* * *

What sets great players apart?

I believe there's one trait that sets great players apart: it's their humility about their outstanding skills. It may be hard to believe, but most of the truly great ones realize they don't have to brag, boast, or pound their chests every time they so something. They appreciate what they can do and how it can help the team, and don't mind sharing the spotlight with others. I've been blessed by several truly great players in my career and here are the attributes I've seen in every one.

1. Highly motivated - Extreme passion for the game.

2. Driven - Outstanding work ethic.

3. Intrinsically motivated - Plays for the accomplishments and moments.

4. Intellectual - Able to see every situation and solution.

5. Goal oriented - Knows where they're headed, and what they want to accomplish.

6. Humble - Concerning their ability.

7. Mentally strong - Never lets the possibility of failing get in the way.

8. Wants the ball with the game on the line - Confident in their ability.

9. Will settle for nothing less than the best from their teammates - Understands everyone has a job to do.

10. Willing to say what needs to be said - Strong Leadership qualities.

11. Recognizes key moments - Knows when it's time to perform.

12. Determined - Will let nothing get in the way.

13. Fearless - Confident in every situation.

14. Highly skilled - Has the skills and tools to get the job done.

15. Calm - Ability to see solutions without emotions at key times.

Do great players define moments, or do moments define great players?

* * *

Hall of Fame Swimming Coach, Dave Barney, vividly offers final instructions in a championship showdown. From his article, "The Magic of Motivation…or Not."

This is going to be the greatest test in your racing life to this point. Embrace the challenge of it all. Indeed, do more than embrace it; relish it, revel in it. It will bring out the very best in you. Appreciate the fact that you are racing one of the state's finest all-time swimmers. But here's how you can win. This is not rocket science. Very simple, as a matter of fact. Most importantly, your opening 50 must beat her to the wall by whatever margin possible. You've simply got to take that opening half of the race out like gangbusters and gain an edge. When you've done that, you must maintain that edge through the third twenty-five. You know all too well what a strong back-half swimmer she is, so it's important not to let her back in the door of that narrowness of edge before the third turn. Simply said, you must hold her at bay during that third length. When you've done that, you will come to perhaps the most critical singular moment of the race itself, the third and final turn. You must focus on it completely. It must be momentous, clean and powerful both going in and coming out, and streamlined to-the-max off the wall, no matter how breathless or tired you may be. Staying down in distance is your business, but breakout powerfully, knowing that you only have a little more than half a pool to the finish. But that's entirely your half-a-pool. Nothing I can say to you now will be of much use to you then in that last fifteen or so yards to the finish. You're on your own, so to speak. And, for what it's worth, I want you to know that I'd much rather it be in your hands and in your heart than in mine. You're a champion . . . a thoroughbred . . . finish like one.

* * *

Great players leave their stamp on a team and program through what they accomplish. While some may say this (or that) player was lucky in scoring, defending, or making a great save to win the game, I'd argue that if you look at their careers, you'll undoubtedly see many situations where they came through. They will always define moments with their ability. Without them, there would be no moments.

Great players have a knack for being in the right place at the right time. They step out of that phone booth with their cape on:

The note simply said, "WE CAN WIN THIS GAME."

About 10 minutes later the note came back, "YES WE CAN."

We were a fairly new team having only established girls' soccer four years earlier, playing against a private school that was clearly superior to us in talent, across the field.

As I sat on the bench watching our JV game, I sent a note across the field to our seniors and particularly to our leader at the time. I always wanted our Varsity players thinking positively about their game as the JV played. The note simply said, "WE CAN WIN THIS GAME." About 10 minutes later the note came back, "YES WE CAN." It was signed by Haley. I knew then that we had a chance and how key she was to our success.

She was a fiery player, dominating the midfield in a 4-3-3 alignment without any help. A tireless performer who gave everything she had in every game, literally coming off exhausted after every contest. If you were going into battle, you'd want her on your side.

The game wore on, and amazingly the score was 0-0 with 19 minutes to go. At that time, a tie would have been a win for us. However, the team we were playing was peppering our goal with shot after shot. Our goalkeeper was doing a phenomenal job stopping everything coming at her. As the clock continued to tick down, you could see the other team was frustrated. With 17 minutes to go, their sweeper drove a ground ball right at us.

Recognizing a key moment, Haley ran onto the ball 25 yards out and struck it with amazing force and accuracy toward their goal. Their goalkeeper was clearly caught off guard and off her line. The ball sailed over her head, clipped the inside of the left post and hit the back of the net for the most phenomenal goal I've ever seen in my career. Our team was ecstatic!

We would go on to protect our lead in the last 17 minutes and pull off the biggest upset of my career. It would not have been possible without Haley recognizing a key moment. She was the first truly great player we had, and it was her determination that made her great. I still have the note, and film of the game which I watch from time to time.

As a coach how do you deal with a great player either individually or with your team? Do you compensate, downplay it, go overboard, tell the team that's the way it is?

I believe the more you highlight a great player, or any player, the more problems you create for yourself. A climate of resentment and jealousy can develop as other players only hear you talk about a certain player every day. Any chemistry your team had is gone. Truly great players don't want to be treated any differently to any other player. They understand their role, what they can do, and are comfortable with it. Treat them like any other member of your team. And remember, they answer to the same rules and expectations as the other players.

I will say you need to let great players do what they do best – play the game. Often we inhibit their natural ability by over-coaching through schemes, formations, and plays.

"Great players are creative and need the freedom to paint their murals on the field. They see moments and situations that no one else does. Let them paint!"

Emphasize humility with great players, every chance you get. Remind them to be thankful for the skill and knowledge they possess. Point out that they need their teammates to be successful, making sure they thank them for a great pass, corner kick, etc. You may or may not recognize truly great players until they've gone. Looking back on their careers, you'll see the great things they accomplished. Remember, superheroes live their lives in secret and only put on their capes when situations look grave. They're humble in that respect, just like your players. Great players are a blessing. Enjoy every minute of their careers.

21. Ten Statements Players Rarely Say to Their Coaches

Communication between you and your players is a key aspect for building a successful program. There will be times when that communication is positive, and times when it's negative. It may be spoken or unspoken.

While every player is different in what motivates or shuts them down, there are common threads with respect to how they want (or expect) to be treated. As a coach, it's important to understand that they may (or may not) vocalize it, but their actions or demeanor may speak volumes. Reading their reactions to certain situations will help you understand what works best, and what doesn't.

In fact, understanding what your players would rarely or never tell you will help you become a better coach.

1. **"Challenge me"** - Players want to grow and improve every day. Progress your practices so that they challenge every player every day.

2. **"Hold me accountable"** - If they step out of line, they expect to suffer the consequences. When they underperform, they need to hear it. You let them down when you let them slide.

3. **"Be tough on me"** - Players want a coach whose expectations are higher than theirs, and a coach who doesn't settle for mediocrity. Be willing to make a point when necessary if they aren't focused.

4. **"Don't be my friend, I have plenty"** - Maintain a professional relationship. Overly-friendly relationships diminish an individual's ability to truly coach a player, and respect is lost.

5. **"Quit making my decisions, I'm ready"** - Players want responsibility, and despise instructions continually shouted from the sidelines. Allow them to grow and make those decisions for themselves.

6. **"Don't praise or ridicule me in front of the team"** - Calling them out in a group will always diminish respect. Talk to individual players away from the team, with an assistant coach.

7. **"Immediate apologies infuriate me"** - Don't apologize immediately if you make a mistake. If you must revisit a moment, explain your logic *after* a period of time and move on. Immediate

apologies lead players to believe you didn't think your initial answer or reaction through.

8. **"Why am I not playing more?"** - Players want to play. Never avoid players who play very little or send them to your assistant coaches. Talk with them every chance you get.

9. **"That decision isn't fair"** - Take the emotion out of your decisions. Every player is watching when you make decisions with respect to expectations, and especially when it's a key player. Consistency is the key.

10. **"Why are we doing this?"** - Explain the "why" of your activities in practice and how it will benefit players as individuals and as a team. Repetition that may seem boring to your players is necessary to develop high levels of skill.

We spend a lot of time evaluating and analyzing our players. How much time do we spend on our communication technique and style? What our players are reluctant or afraid to share is very important. It allows us to think about areas of communication we can improve.

The statements listed above are very realistic. Over the course of a career, I've heard them all from players not afraid to tell me what they thought, which I appreciated! Did such feedback make me happy? Absolutely not, but it did allow me to grow and become a better coach.

We can learn a lot from our players. I did. Take the time to listen, whether the words are spoken or not.

22. Coaching Responsibilities

There is so much to consider when you get that first coaching job, so here follows a list of areas that you should be involved in as your career begins. While it may be impossible for you to do them all, you should be aware of what is going on in each one. Delegating some responsibility to your assistants, parents, and players will help.

By putting your stamp on each one, you begin that road that leads to a culture of success in a program you can be proud of.

Supervision/safety of players - When the first player arrives until the last player leaves they are your responsibility. This is every situation: after a game, practice, after a bus ride on an away game, etc. Never leave a student alone or let them ride with someone else without parents' verified permission.

Announcing the starting date for practice - Use social media/team website/the local paper to make an announcement for the start date of practice, what to bring, and what is required. Include your email address and phone number for those who may want to contact you. (Ask a parent to be your media expert and take care of these responsibilities.)

Pre-season meeting agenda

1. Introduce yourself and your coaches to all in attendance.
2. Thank everyone for being there.
3. Explain the philosophy and vision for the program.
4. Go over player expectations, rules, requirements and accountability.
5. Remind parents/players of location(s) and the times of all practices/ games.
6. Explain the process of notification should plans change.
7. Go over what players need before and during practice.
8. Cover what fees are required for participation/uniforms/trips, etc.
9. Detail procedures should a player be injured during practice or games.
10. Explain the disciplinary outcomes that may result in a player sitting out of a game.

11. Go over the 24-hour rule of approaching a coach concerning participation/issues.

12. Questions/Concerns.

13. Thank everyone for being there.

Expenses for participation - Prior to tryouts, prepare a list of estimated expenses for each player for the season. Make copies and go over this at your pre-season meeting with parents. Be ready to justify everything listed.

Team communications - Designate a parent to be the information officer of your team. They can manage the team website and all the social media team sites. Working together, you can readily get information out when needed such as when practice has to be changed.

Appropriate communications - It is always prudent to know that all team-related communications are considered public records and remember, a coach should never exchange text messages or emails of a personal nature with a player.

Notifications to students/parents - Each head coach is responsible for distributing pre-season forms required by the state association to each prospective student-athlete, and parents, as well as forms required by the school board. Hand everything out at the pre-season meeting, and define a deadline for their return.

Coach/parent relationship - Parents can be a positive part of any athletic program. Introduce yourself and encourage them to take on key roles for the team. Express your expectations up front and be consistent. Parents who take ownership in the program will bring other parents onboard.

Cutting players - On the first day of tryouts, let players know exactly how they will be evaluated and the procedure for letting them know if they made the team or not. I recommend meeting face to face with every player after tryouts, especially the ones who don't make the team. They put in the effort, so respect that by talking to them. There is always something positive you can share about who they are.

Budgeting - Each sport has a budget with a seasonal allocation. Find the amount on your first day from your Athletic Director. Decide what the priorities are, then get them approved and ordered. Every purchase has to be approved by the AD, the Principal, and the school board. Never order anything on your own without approval.

Scheduling - Work within your school's guidelines to schedule games which impact your players' academics the least. Avoid back-to-back games and ones that don't allow your team proper recovery time. Set up your schedule to best challenge your team. A veteran group needs the toughest schedule; young teams need easier early-season opponents to build confidence.

Eligibility - Check your players' grades once a week. Most schools have a grade check system allowing AD's to see if all players are eligible for each week's game. Visit teachers and let them know you expect the best from your players in their class. Get in early with players who are struggling to make the grade. Players who transfer to your school should get proper paperwork from the AD. They won't be allowed to practice or play until that paperwork is approved by the school and state association.

Hosting tournaments - Bring the top teams to your area for a pre-season showcase or midseason tournament. Charge teams an entry fee to help offset the cost, and turn the concessions, etc. over to your booster organization. Ask your Athletic Director if your team can have 100% of the revenue. It's a wonderful way to promote your community and facilities.

Game officials - Meet and greet officials at every game whether home or away. Developing a respectful relationship with officials builds rapport and ultimately defines your team in their eyes. Knowing them will open doors during a game if communication is necessary. Remember they have a tough job as well.

Transportation of team - Most coaches are required to fill out bus requests for away games and get those to the transportation department. These must be approved by the Athletic Director. Complete them before the season so you can move on to more pressing matters. You may at some point want to earn your CDL or Commercial Driving License enabling you to drive the team if needed.

Media - Work with the local media to promote your team. Get to know the local reporters and develop a good relationship. Avoid an interview right after a tough loss when emotions are high. Ask your assistant to stand in if needed. Take credit for losses and give credit to your players in a win when at the microphone or being quoted. Saying a few good words about your opponent is prudent as well.

Awards - Decide what awards are most important for the end of year banquet, and attend all coaches meetings where players are voted on for All-State, All-Region, and All-American. Representing your players should always be a priority. Midseason and end of year tournaments will require you to select all-tournament players. It is always tough to highlight individuals in a team sport.

Fundraising - Work with boosters as much as possible to raise money for the team. Show them your dedication and willingness to roll up your sleeves and do anything to assist the team.

Reporting a player injury - You may be responsible for completing an accident report should a player be injured at practice or in a game, even if a trainer is there. After proper care is administered for the player, check with the trainer to see if they are going to do it or whether you have to. Most schools require this within three days of the injury.

Heat Index - Safety at practice during hot summer months is of the utmost importance. Be aware that during summer pre-season months your trainer may shut outside practice down due to the heat index being high. Immediately take your players to shade or inside where there is air conditioning. Do your best to schedule practices early in the morning or late in the evening, give plenty of water breaks, and check with your trainer for the heat index forecast for a particular day.

Camps - Consider offering a youth camp at your field in the off-season, and take your team to a university team camp right before your practice begins. Use some of your players at the youth camp as instructors. It's a great way to work with future players and have fun as well. Team Camp is a wonderful way to get your team away from home and work on team building and leadership activities.

State Association guidelines/rules - Bookmark the web address of your state association in case you need to check on rules, requirements, tournament guidelines, etc. Introduce yourself to the administrator that covers your sport, and develop a positive working relationship.

Planning off-season training - After the season is over, list all the areas the team needs to work on while it's fresh in your mind. Prioritize what you want your players to accomplish and improve during the off-season. Set up dates, have a team meeting, and get them motivated to get started.

Coaching education - Attend every seminar, convention and/or course possible for your sport. Most have the best clinicians and teachers, and you'll leave inspired and energized ready to begin the season with renewed energy. Get with your AD and ask him for financial support to develop your skills.

Equipment requisition - Work with your AD on purchasing equipment and uniforms during the off-season. Assist him or her by getting bids on the specific items you need. All items will have to be approved by the AD and the Principal.

Inventory - Keep a list of every piece of equipment owned by your sport and team. You'll be asked to fill out an inventory form at the end of each season. I also recommend taking pictures as well.

Equipment storage - With your players, make sure game and practice equipment are taken apart, portable goals broken down, nets taken off, and all balls, cones, etc. are stored inside for the off-season.

Field Maintenance - The school's maintenance department (or an outside contractor) will make sure your field is mowed, etc. However, you'll probably be responsible for stripping it and getting it game ready. Work with your boosters to get this done, and report any problems to your AD. I recommend checking the field a day or two before a game to avoid any last-minute issues on game day.

* * *

Karen Vanover, former Athletic Director and Coach at Lafayette High School gives us four keys to being an effective coach.

In my career as a coach, athletic director, and coach trainer, I've found there are four key ways new coaches can quickly make the best possible contribution:

1. Read/study

This may sound obvious to some, but get informed about your sport through multiple media sources. Having played does not mean you can successfully coach a team in that sport. Read your state, county and school's athletic guides. The guidelines and rules in those documents have been put together by coaches, teachers, principals, athletic directors and superintendents who have had experience with student-athletes and are intended to protect the athlete and you as a coach. Be able to distinguish which are "guidelines" and which ones are hard "rules."

Read the official rulebook for your sport. If you have insomnia it will help you fall asleep because it is so dry, but if you have a situation with a rule and you are informed, it can win a game. Being knowledgeable of the rules will also help you maintain your job. Coaching is not a time to "ask forgiveness rather than permission." "I didn't know" is not acceptable – it is your job to know.

Take your team to camp! How will this make you a better coach? Several ways – you'll learn lots of new ideas, drills, and knowledge from other coaches about the X's and O's of your sport. You will also see others interact with your players and maybe see new ways to teach them and get the most from every player. Another plus is when that other coach tells your players the same thing you've been telling them, they finally realize that you just might know what you are talking about.

2. Make a personal investment in your sport

Join the local, state and national associations for your sport and get involved in them by attending meetings, clinics, camps, conferences and being on boards or committees when possible. Aside from the speakers who are knowledgeable in your sport, the networking with other coaches is invaluable. You will learn that other coaches have the same obstacles as you and you will learn how they are working to solve those problems (and often how NOT to do it).

The first year that I joined the state association, I attended the annual state conference and met many people who had been "voices on the phone." The next fall, our football team was headed to the State playoffs. What should have been an exciting time for me and the head coach was rather stressful as we tried to find money to get turf shoes required to play on artificial turf in the playoffs. Out of the blue, I got a call from an AD I'd met the previous spring who offered us the use of their team's turf shoes. Without that networking and personal contact at the conference, I'm not sure he would have offered.

3. Get involved with your school

Many coaches are not teachers in the school and even if you are, getting involved in your school is important for many reasons. It should be kept in mind that this is a SCHOOL SPORT, not a club sport or "all star" team that athletes pay to be part of. Coaching or being on a school team gives you more than just team membership, it gives you a feeling of belonging. In or out of uniform, the athlete and the coach are representing the school. Participation on the school team is a privilege not a right, therefore, maintaining membership on this team usually holds the athlete to higher standards of conduct and grades.

Attending other functions at the school will help teachers and students recognize who you are and show that you are supporting the school and students outside of your sport. Teachers who recognize you will be more likely to address behavior and/or grade problems with you. Your players will enjoy seeing you off the court/field as well.

Getting to know the other coaches at the school will open up a valuable resource for you. The experienced ones, especially, will be glad to help you if you ask (and many you won't even have to ask). Knowing the other coaches will also be helpful when you have to share facilities, share athletes, and can help in shared supervision in the off-season. Networking here can be valuable as well.

4. Communicate

I've rarely heard from players, parents, principals or athletic directors that a coach is communicating too much. Being organized from the beginning will limit the amount of communication necessary. By turning in your team roster, game schedule, practice schedule and other required forms on time and sticking to it, players, parents, and the AD will be well informed. As a new coach, this can be harder than you'd think so if you need help, ask for it. The paperwork can be overwhelming if you don't stay on top of it. Not turning in some forms can result in penalties from the state organization and can be a factor in eligibility and the possibility of having to forfeit games.

* * *

Hall of Fame Volleyball Coach, Jean Kesterson, details a coach's "To Do List"

#1 SWOT Analysis (Strengths/Weaknesses/Opportunities/Threats)

- Do one every year
- Compare at the end of the season
- Compare with other year's SWOT

Strengths - List at least five internal

- coaching staff
- players
- support staff
- athletic department
- school administration
- faculty
- school community
- local community

Weaknesses -List at least five internal

- coaching staff
- players
- support staff
- athletic department
- school administration
- faculty
- school community

Opportunities - List at least three external

- Local community
- Various media outlets
- Your opponents
- Your schedule
- Rules & Classification changes

Threats - List at least three external

- school community
- local community
- various media outlets
- your opponents
- Rules & classification changes

What did you learn from your SWOT analysis?

- What are you going to do about it?
- What can you control?
- What can you not control?

#2 It's a Process

- Set GOALS for each phase of your season
- Plan, plan, plan and then be ready for the unexpected
- Write it down; you look like you know what you're doing.
- Everyone involved
- Focus on your next opponent, but coaches are planning for state

#3 Have a Vision

- Have a quality staff
- Everyone has a role in the program
- Specialization speeds success
    - Coaches
    - Players
- Don't reinvent the wheel
    - Ask winners

#4 Great Kids = Great Team

- Great kids make it easier to produce a great team
- Everyone has a role. Communicate it to them.
- A shared vision with all parties involved
- Speak it into existence
- Fake it until you make it

#5 Lead Parents

- **YOU** pick one for each team in the program
- Have a binder with a timetable and responsibilities of parents
- You communicate with the one head parent
- He/she communicates to team parent
- They communicate to parents on specific team

#6 Teach Leadership

#7 Write Down your Team Goals

- Goals are
    - Specific
    - Measurable
    - Action Oriented
    - Realistic
    - Timely
- Have goals that scare you!

#8 Feed the Beast

- Tell the WORLD
    - PrepVolleyball.com, MaxPreps, local media
    - Social Media

#9 Give Feedback

- VERY important for Gen Z
- Let them know you care about their best interest

#10 Have Fun

- Your energy is contagious

* * *

23. Coaching Requirements and Code of Conduct

Before you apply for a coaching job, contact the school's administrative office and inquire about the requirements. Below is an example of what may be required. Don't become discouraged if you don't meet all the criteria. Contact the Athletic Director, or someone you may know at the school, show interest and learn more about the position and the climate surrounding the program. Doing your research before an interview may give you a much-needed advantage, and could make you aware of issues which underlie why this may (or may not) be the right job.

You may want to become a head coach immediately without any experience. While this shows initiative, it may put you in a tough situation as you lack the necessary experience to lead a team. Think about applying for, and becoming, an assistant; it will offer you the time and experience to prepare for a head coaching position.

Sample coaching requirements (soccer)

Before securing a coaching position, you'll need to meet certain requirements, have a contract with the school, and be approved by the state association office.

*Head Coach:

1. College Degree.
2. Two years of Head Coaching Experience or USSF "B" License or NSCAA Premier Diploma.
3. Professional Teacher's Certificate OR NFHS Fundamentals of Coaching Course passed prior to coaching.
4. Three personal references.
5. Background Check before coaching.
6. Board of Education approval prior to coaching.
7. Successful completion of a Concussion Course, and review of current concussion information.
8. Completion of the State Sports-Specific Online Rules Review each season.
9. Successful completion of a First Aid course before coaching and renewed every two years.

10. Successful completion of CPR/AED training prior to coaching and renewed every year.

11. College playing experience desired.

*Assistant Coach:

1. Completion of 48 or more college credit hours before coaching.

2. One year coaching experience or USSF "D" License or NSCAA National Diploma.

3. A Professional Teacher's Certificate OR NFHS Fundamentals of Coaching Course (online) passed prior to the second year of coaching.

4. Three personal references.

5. Background Check before coaching.

6. Board of Education approval prior to coaching.

7. Completion of a Concussion Course, and review of current concussion information.

8. Completion of the State Sports-Specific Online Rules Review each season.

9. Successful completion of a First Aid Course and renewed every two years.

10. Successful completion of CPR/AED training and renewed every year.

*Your school or state association's requirements may vary. During the interview, ask for their specific requirements for head coach and assistant coach roles.

The above is only an example of what might be required.

Coaches' code of conduct

Every school will have a version of the "Coaches' Code of Conduct" like the one listed below. A coach's responsibilities are varied and many, but you must always have a high standard of character and integrity for yourself and your team. Every time you step on the field you represent yourself, your family, and your school, and your actions will be under close scrutiny.

In a tension-filled game, emotions can get out of control. Always remember your team is a reflection of you, and you're the role model they look to. Keep in mind all the points listed here as a guideline for everything you represent, and understand that your signature binds you to act accordingly.

Coach's sample code of conduct - It is the responsibility of a coach to educate student-athletes through participation in sport. Coaches must teach players the skills of the sport as well as sportsmanship and fair play both on and off the field. Coaches are responsible for the conduct of all players and members of the coaching staff at practices, plus before, during, and after games or events.

On and off the field or court, the coach will:

Provide supervision of all players, both on and off the field, at all times while the players are under his or her care.

- Show respect to officials, teammates, opposing team players, coaches, and spectators.

- Greet officials and the opposing coach to set a positive tone for the game.

- Promote fair play and high standards of behavior.

- Promote good sportsmanship by athletes and spectators.

- Serve as a role model for players, coaches, and opposing team members.

- Prevent and/or report negative initiation practices and hazing.

- Treat all players with respect and dignity.

- Protect the health and safety of his/her players.

- Be aware that he or she has a tremendous influence on the student-athlete, and shall never place the value of winning above instilling the highest ideals of character.

- Uphold the honor and dignity of the profession. In all personal contact with student-athletes, officials, Athletic Directors, school administrators, the media and the public, the coach will set an example of the highest ethical and moral conduct.

- Take a strong leadership role in the prevention of bullying, hazing, drug, alcohol and tobacco abuse.

- Promote all sports programs of the school and direct his or her team in alignment with the total sports program.

- Respect and support officials. The coach will never indulge in behavior that incites players or spectators to act disrespectfully against the officials.

- Never exert pressure or influence on any faculty members to give student athletes special treatment.

- Exert his or her influence to enhance sportsmanship from spectators, both directly and by working closely with cheerleaders, pep club sponsors, booster clubs, and administrators.

Coach's Name _____

Signature: _____

Date: _____

24. Do You Have a Coaching Philosophy?

Do you have a Coaching Philosophy? Have you put it into words and looked at it? It may be time to do that, and look at who you are and what you believe as a coach. We spend a lot of time evaluating players, and their strengths and weaknesses, but do we take the time to evaluate ourselves?

As a new coach, a philosophy is usually based on experiences as a player, remembering how coaches handled or mishandled certain situations. That can be a challenge since we all remember things from a certain perspective and don't always see the whole picture.

I've heard the following statement several times from some of my former players who are now coaching, "I can't get anything out of my team. When I played, I always practiced and played hard."

They are right. They did practice and play hard, but their focus at the time was their own work ethic. As a player, they never had to try to motivate those players who give less than 100% or who are mediocre at times. Now, as a coach, they have to see and work with the bigger picture.

"When you are a player, all you have to do is think about your own game, your fitness, your diet, etc. – you train, you go home, and that's it. But when you become a manager, you have to think about the physical and mental preparation of the whole squad, building up team spirit, being aware of medical issues. Above all, you have to develop your leadership skills." Fabio Capello

Other coaches develop their philosophy as an assistant or a head coach, on the job. In the early years of their career, they piece it together experience after experience until they've built a set of expectations. This approach can be precarious, especially while you're learning, since your current team may not know what to expect in different situations because of an uncertain philosophy.

It's better to think through the big picture right away and construct a philosophy to work from, even if you might wind up changing it as needed.

Here are some guiding principles to keep in mind:

- What do you want your team and players to learn?

- What will you expect and what won't you tolerate?

- How will you relate to your players?

- What environment will you create for the players?
- What style of play will your teams be known for?

"You must love the game and want to share with the players a certain way of life, a way of seeing soccer." Arsene Wenger

Consider five areas when developing your philosophy.

1. **Expectations/Discipline** - Players and parents, leadership, goal setting, being positive, teamwork, attitude, competition.

2. **Training** - Technical, tactical, psychological, and fitness.

3. **Game Strategy** - Offensive, defensive, set plays, etc.

4. **Motivation** - Yours and theirs: intrinsic, extrinsic.

5. **Character and Values** - Decisions and leadership based on what is right.

Looking at each more closely:

Expectations/Discipline - This is the foundation that will define you and your team. Think about what you can tolerate and what you can't. It sets the tone for your style of leadership, and I suggest, if possible, that it's developed *with* the team. When expectations are set with the team, athletes have ownership and are more likely to follow them. This area also includes school rules such as grades, drugs, alcohol, class conduct, etc., as well as being on time to games and practices, attitude, goal setting, teamwork, and parental expectations.

"Based on history the expectations are simply the highest, it kind of could become a burden for you or it could be something that you are really proud of, you know, so I take the second one." Jurgen Klinsmann

Training - Are you concerned with development or winning? Are you a sculptor or a blender? It really depends on the level you coach. Certainly, at younger or inexperienced levels, the emphasis should be on development. Do you build players up or do you break them down in an effort to bring them back up? Is team building a priority? What about fitness? Do you train your team more with the ball, without the ball, or 50/50, 60/40? How will you break practices down? Do you plan or improvise?

Game Strategy – Using soccer as an example, are your teams defined by their defending, attacking, possession, or strong midfield play? What formation do you put your team in? How will you attack and defend corner kicks, free kicks, playing out of the back? How do you attack different formations? How do you defend certain formations? Will you defend zonally or utilize man-to-man marking? Are you playing to win, or playing now in an effort to win later? What situations are you trying to exploit on the field? How do you approach the game in certain situations?

Motivation - What ideas do you have to motivate your team? Is your motivation positive or negative? What inspires your team? What inspires you? How will you handle losing attitudes? Do you punish your team for mistakes in practice? Or wait for a teachable moment when they've executed the skill or play masterfully? Do you provide a competitive environment for players to be challenged and improve in? How will you get your team ready to play against a top opponent? A weak opponent? What is your passion?

Character and Values - This area is certainly interwoven into the previous categories and will play a big role in your career. Your decisions, to a large extent, will be based on what values you were taught by your parents, teachers, and coaches. Winning and losing is never the reason to get into coaching. Rather, it's the difference you will make in a young person's life in a positive way. The ability to assist a young person with their challenges and struggles on the field and in the classroom is the most rewarding, means the most, and will last longer than any trophy. When we base our decisions on strong character and values, we can rest assured that we made the best decision possible. You may not always make the most popular decision, but make sure it is the right one. As a coach, you need that rock to lean on in tough times.

"I do not think it is fair to judge coaches purely on results. You have to see how they work, judge their philosophy and assess their relationship with the players." Louis Van Gaal

Your style of coaching will dictate how you implement your philosophy and ultimately how your team responds. That philosophy should always be adapting, and never stagnant. It's a good idea to revisit your philosophy from time to time, seeing how it's changed, and contemplating the need for change. A philosophy based on character and values will always carry you through challenging times in my view.

Your philosophy ultimately will define your legacy. When everything else is stripped away, including wins, losses, player recognition, your recognition, tough times and great times, your philosophy shows who you are and who you were.

By formulating it now, you're on your way to a successful and rewarding career and program.

LEADERSHIP COMPONENTS
Building A Successful Sports Program

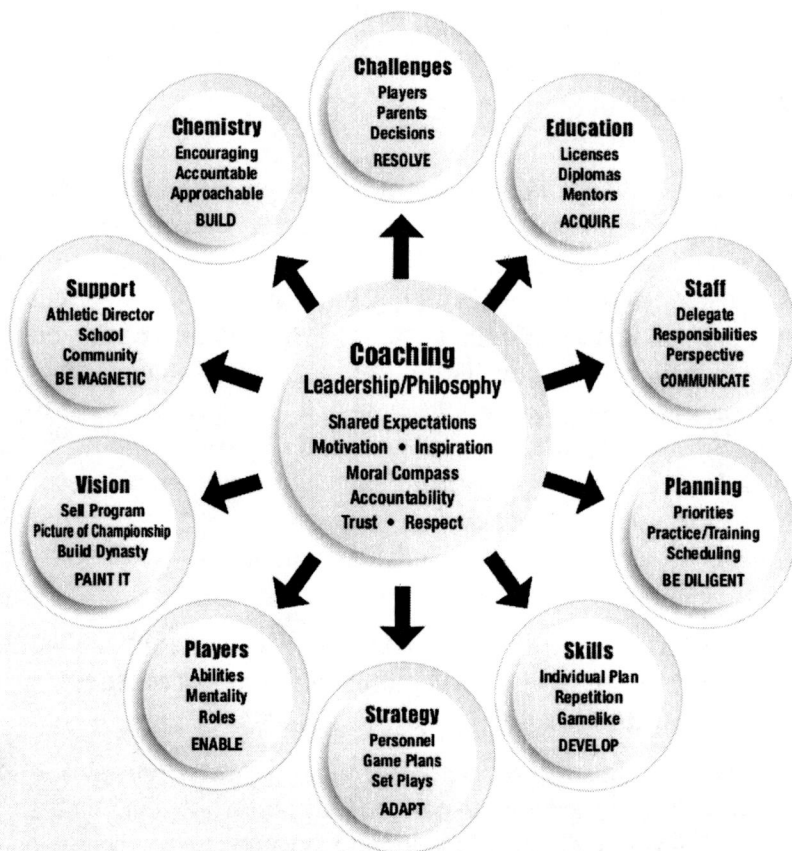

Challenges
Players
Parents
Decisions
RESOLVE

Chemistry
Encouraging
Accountable
Approachable
BUILD

Education
Licenses
Diplomas
Mentors
ACQUIRE

Support
Athletic Director
School
Community
BE MAGNETIC

Staff
Delegate
Responsibilities
Perspective
COMMUNICATE

Coaching
Leadership/Philosophy
Shared Expectations
Motivation • Inspiration
Moral Compass
Accountability
Trust • Respect

Vision
Sell Program
Picture of Championship
Build Dynasty
PAINT IT

Planning
Priorities
Practice/Training
Scheduling
BE DILIGENT

Players
Abilities
Mentality
Roles
ENABLE

Strategy
Personnel
Game Plans
Set Plays
ADAPT

Skills
Individual Plan
Repetition
Gamelike
DEVELOP

Wiser Sports Leadership

25. What Are Your Coaching Principles?

In every aspect of our life, we make decisions based on our beliefs and values. Those can be mainly from how we were raised, our environment and experiences, as well as other factors. Coaching is no different. As a coach, you will be called on to make decisions that impact individuals as well as your team. Those decisions, while not always the same with respect to each situation, must be fair. **Leadership Principles assist us through the decision making process.**

My leadership principles fit into four main categories:

Definitions from dictionary.com

Character - "The mental and moral qualities distinctive to an individual."

Integrity - "The quality of being honest, having strong moral principles."

Resoluteness - "Firm or determined; unwavering."

Forgiveness - "The action or process of forgiving or being forgiven."

Character - The strength we have to draw on in tough decisions is based on our character. It's who we really are. Character may not win any popularity contests, but when our players and parents turn to us, it allows us to make sound choices based on what is right. Never waiver or defer decisions that are required of you. By showing a willingness to step up and lead in moments of uncertainty, a new respect will be earned.

The right decision is never one you'll lose sleep over.

"Where's Kendra?" I asked my assistant coach as the JV game was nearing kickoff.

"She's over in the bleachers with the varsity team," she replied.

I couldn't believe it. Kendra had been out with an injury for several games. I told her at a previous game that we'd play her in a few JV games for limited minutes to get her comfortable on the ball again. To me, what I said was clear, but why wasn't she with the JV team warming up? Upset, I asked one of our managers to go get her. When she arrived, I asked her if she had understood our plan. She said yes, but her parent had told her she wasn't playing JV.

Wow!

Knowing the parent wasn't at our field, I asked her to call him and have him join us. When the parent arrived, he explained that Kendra didn't want to play JV, and he thought it was degrading. I explained the most effective way to regain her playing form was to play in several JV games to get her game-ready for the varsity. He said he would rather wait for her to just play varsity. We only had six games left, and we needed her back as soon as possible. It wasn't possible without extra work in the minimal time available. Our team would pay the price because a player wouldn't do what was best for the team, and ultimately what was best for her. But my decision was clear. I couldn't play her because she wouldn't be ready.

Integrity - Integrity is on display every day. Looking the other way in any situation that is wrong (regardless of whether it involves you or your team, or not) is wrong. To me, integrity is your backbone, your willingness to separate right from wrong. If your intuition tells you something just isn't right, it's usually correct.

Situations may involve one of your players who doesn't live in your district; they are failing a class, skipping school, and you need to decide whether to play them or not. Alternatively, it could involve being lured into accepting benefits for personal gain that are outside the rules. Likewise, what will you do if you know another coach is violating rules?

Your integrity is reflected in every decision and action of you and your program. Your career is on the line, and if you look the other way, you stand to lose everything. However, the greatest lesson is that your players are watching everything you do and a bad example can never be undone. Be a shining example of what a coach should stand for. ***Stand for all that is right - your players are watching.***

Resoluteness - In my coaching career, I've heard the following statement from players many times, "Coach, I know what I did was wrong, and I promise it won't happen again." It's usually followed up with, "Can you please not sit me out or suspend me?" Moments like this will define your relationship with your players and your team. If your expectations are clear and have been explained to the players, the decision must always be the same: they have to pay for their behavior. Not because you're a tough coach, but because changing expectations would undermine your ability to lead. If that should happen, you have lost your team.

Remember to be unwavering in your decisions irrespective of whether it's a star player or a player that plays very little. Those expectations are for everyone. ***Never compromise your beliefs and values.***

* * *

Great example of resoluteness from Coach Aaron Ocampo, Head Football Coach, Centennial High School, Las Cruces, New Mexico

In the 2010 football season, we had to replace quite a lot of seniors from the 09 team that lost on a two-point conversion in the state semifinals to the eventual state champion. We had very few returning starters, but we had a few very competitive seniors that led our team. We lost the second game of the season to a team that was probably not as good as us, but went on to win the next few games. We were finding our way as a team and improving every week. That was one of our main objectives for the season (improving every week).

We were coming into our fifth game of the season and were playing an up and coming power in our state, that had a future D I quarterback. They were undefeated and playing very well. Our team was excited at the challenge of playing them on their homecoming.

We had a running back named Anthony, a talented junior who showed a lot of promise as a football player. Unfortunately, he didn't take the classroom very seriously. He was always on the edge of not meeting the academic requirement to play. During the week of the game, he missed a practice. Our team policy is that you must practice in order to play in the game. I chose to stand by our policy even though the game was a very big game. I didn't let him play in the game, nor did I travel him to the game. I knew that it was better to stand by our core values, rather than fudge the rules, so we could go into the game with one of our top players.

We had to move a wide receiver to the running back position for a lot of the game. It was a challenge to game plan for the week because we had to shuffle so many people around, but the rest of our players stepped up to the challenge and we came out and competed well in the first half. To my surprise, we were winning 14-7 at halftime. This is when the game turned really strange. There was a lightning delay lasting two hours. The other team came out hot, but we battled back and made a great game out of it. We ended up winning by causing a fumble at our own four-yard line to prevent the other team from taking the lead. We were very excited to hand this team their only loss during the regular season.

It was one of those moments, as a coach, that made me proud how our players battled adversity. Most of all, we stepped up to the challenge of competing well without one of our best players. It really showed our team that being a team player and a "winner" is more important than being a star. Anthony ended up coming back with a good attitude and playing well for the rest of the season. As a senior, he ended up making the All-State football team. His grades improved slightly, but his commitment level was much better from that point on. Choosing to stick to our values turned out to be something that helped our entire team. I feel we would have done just as well had we lost the game. That team ended up winning the rest of the regular season's games and advanced to the state championship game. We lost in the state championship, but we had a special season, especially considering the number of returners we had at the beginning of the season.

Like we tell our team, do the right thing and focus on the "process" of being a champion and the scoreboard will take care of itself.

* * *

Forgiveness - In coaching, it may be easy to hold a grudge. Whether it's another coach who ran the score up on you, said something you didn't agree with, or who talks down to you. It might be a player who just doesn't listen to you the way you wish. It could be a parent who continually complains about everything you do for their child and is not shy about telling you what a lousy coach you are. It could be an administrator who reminds you of your duties and what you need to accomplish to keep your job. I could go on and on, but I know you get the picture.

As a coach, you have to be the bigger man or woman, and forgive them and move on. Of the people I mentioned, you have very little control over parents, other coaches, and administrators. You do have control over your players, but not always 100%. Learn to forgive them for their shortcomings and mistakes, just as you make mistakes every day as well. When you do that, you'll be a lot happier and a better coach. Always remember to forgive yourself in situations where you know you didn't give your best. Moving on is an important aspect of coaching.

The art of forgiving allows you to live.

Base your career on sound principles that will guide you when times are challenging. Some decisions are tougher than others, but knowing you did the right thing even though it wasn't popular is comforting. Remember to be clear in your expectations, and understand we've all made mistakes, and those mistakes usually come with a price.

Coaching is leading, and leading is never easy.

26. Humility, Embrace It

Have you ever got caught up feeling really good about what you've achieved, whether it's the game last night or your career so far? I'm pretty sure we've all revisited successful events and felt great satisfaction about our ability to make key decisions that impacted outcomes.

Very often, we think too highly of ourselves as a result of congratulations from others, awards we receive, and our egos. It's a common trap for coaches, and just when we think we've found the holy grail of motivation, strategy or new plays, that word – humility – finds a way to bring us back to reality.

My colleague and I spend a lot of time talking about a fierce rivalry game played each year in our area. We agree that win or lose, we feel like we have a sign on our chest that says, "We Won," or "We Lost." As coaches, we believe everyone in the state, our town, our friends, as well as our fellow coaches, care about and know the score of our game.

The day after my rivalry game, I was in a local store when I saw an old friend. I was still pumped over the big win as we talked and relived some memories. At some point in the conversation I thought for sure he was about to congratulate me. Instead, he said, "Now where is it you're working?" Are you kidding me! He didn't know I guided my team to victory last night, or care about the big game? Humility had appeared out of nowhere, like a back screen in basketball.

How can we, as coaches, stay grounded and still enjoy the jubilation of great games and events with our teams?

- Accept congratulations and accolades, don't wear them.

- Understand coaching is about the players, not you.

- Keep in mind that your game may not be that important to others. Families have other obligations.

- Remember that not everyone knows who you are, or what you've accomplished.

- Seek recognition for your players and team, but seldom for yourself.

- Take comfort that winning or losing will never define who you really are as a coach.

- Dedicate yourself to the task, not the reward.

- Remind yourself that others coached before you, and others will coach after you.

I was sitting with a coaching friend one day during our combined classes at school. He had just won a prestigious state coaching award. As we talked, one of his students came by and said, "Coach, I saw where you won that coach of the county thing. Congratulations." We just looked at each other, and knew at that moment humility had walked by. He felt as I would have, that everyone knew that he was the district coach of the year, a supreme recognition by his peers. In reality, awards and accolades for us mean very little to others. Humility...

Humility can show up at different times, but very often it shines brightest after a loss. We may be on a winning streak, or have won our district or region for the past several years, and grown complacent. There's a sense of being the best coach ever, or believing we've figured out how to be successful. That's when humility appears.

We had won 15 games in a row with two left to play in the regular season. All the parents, students and teachers at school had heaped praise on me and our team. This was uncharted waters with no team in our school history doing this well. We thought we had it all figured out and were the best team in the state. The reality was the fact that we hadn't faced a really tough schedule. Our next two games against big city teams would tell us where we stood. We lost both, and were never really in either game. Ironically, a dose of humility turned out to be our motivation. We went on to win the district, region, and one game in the state tournament to finish a great year.

Humility can be viewed by some as a weakness. That school of thought is based on the assumption you have to be strong, tough, and vocal, or others will run all over you. Let's remember that we can be all those and more *and* remain humble. Remembering where you came from, who you are, what you stand for, and what it will take to be successful are all traits of humility. It isn't a word that is used often or emphasized with a lot of coaches, but when you coach from (or to) the heart, you can't avoid it.

Remember, embrace it along the way, or it will embrace you.

There's a movie I highly recommend called, "The Cinderella Man." It's the true story of Max Baer, former Heavyweight Boxing Champion, who during the Great Depression exemplified humility through his efforts to support his family and keep his dream alive, with little thought of himself. Truly a shining example of humility and courage you'll never forget.

27. Pressure to Succeed

suc·ceed [*suh* k-seed] "to accomplish what is attempted or intended." (Dictionary.com)

We constantly feel the pressure to succeed. But what exactly is our definition of that term? In some programs, it involves the need to win every game, every championship. Anything less is perceived as failure. But whose perception is this? Is it truly *our* failure or simply the pressure we feel from another source or sources? Another program's ability to succeed may be winning 50 percent of their games, while some other may define success as the total development of their players.

In a day when social media holds up every mistake or misstep a program or coach makes, we certainly are under the microscope. Can we control that? I don't think so. So what *can* we do? Here are a number of areas to consider:

What boat are you the captain of? The history and tradition of a strong program will bring added pressures with it. Be ready for the first wave to hit, and stand tall for what you believe in. There may be other waves. Be visible and realistic in what you say when asked.

Outside sources will have their opinions - Never get involved, or allow your team to get involved or comment, on opinions in social media. Usually, those making the comments are just venting and have no background as a coach or player for it. "When you wrestle with the pig you both get muddy."

What is your priority? Your job is to put the best team on the field or court. That is your priority. Take time to explain to players what is important and what isn't. Lead your team by example with integrity.

Establish goals for yourself and your team - Prioritize what you want to accomplish for the season and with the team. Establish realistic goals that can be met, along with some challenging goals.

Stand tall - Never change your style of coaching based on pressure from outside sources that aren't affiliated with your team. That said, evaluate what your team is accomplishing and prove willing to adapt things if they are out of control.

Be true to your boss - You only answer to those who hired you. As long as they are satisfied with your performance, continue with your direction.

Comparisons are apples and oranges - Getting caught up with success or perceived success by other coaches and teams is a no-win situation.

Your situation is unique and different from theirs. It's not fair to you or your team to make comparisons. Stay focused on your situation.

Never hide - When things are going badly, never bail out. Prepare, show-up and answer questions, even though it might be tough. You'll never regret doing the right thing.

Lay your head on your pillow - When all is said and done, win or lose, or when dealing with tough situations, be able to lay your head on your pillow and know you did the right thing for your team to be successful.

* * *

A great example from Coach Mike Bowlin, 2016 District Football Coach of the Year, East Jessamine High

When I began my head coaching career in the early 2000's, I was coaching football at a program that had very limited success in its past. Being very ambitious and naive I was sure that my coaching style, knowledge and work ethic would be all it would take to turn this program into a winner.

Before I ever coached my first game, I had a player fail a mandatory drug test. This player was fast, strong, athletic and had been a three year starter. He was slated to be a starter in every aspect of the game for our team. His attitude had never been great, and his work ethic was subpar. He simply got by on talent.

By school policy, he was to sit out for the first four games of the season. In my heart, I knew that his involvement in drugs should eliminate him from the team. I did not sleep well. As a rookie in this position, I gave in to his ability and the temptation to win. We simply couldn't put anybody on the field with as much talent as him. I made my mind up that when he returned in the fifth week of the season, he would go right back into the lineup. Sleepless night after sleepless night followed that decision.

We were winless through four games and three of those contests had gone down to the wire. I kept thinking that if we had this one star things might be different. When week five finally came along, I put him back in the lineup. On his first carry, he fumbled. On the first series of defense, he gave up a touchdown pass. He took himself out of the game on a kickoff and left the team with only 10 men on the field at one point. I could feel the rest of the team staring at me. At this moment I realized I had made a terrible mistake. The players quit playing hard that night, and for the first time all season we got blown out.

My original gut instinct was that he should not come back. His attitude and work ethic was a glaring sign that he be dismissed even before the failed test. I gave in to temptation of talent. What I failed to realize was that even though the other players were not as talented, they had bought into what I was saying. They believed that effort, attitude, aggressiveness, and attention to detail could win the day. Now they saw me as a fake. I had lost their belief in what I was saying. The star stood for nothing that I believed in. He was simply blessed with athletic ability.

Ability does not make you a winner. We floundered through the season and won two games. I vowed from that point forward that I would never let the temptation of talent ever let me lose sight of right and wrong. Almost exactly two years later, a very similar situation arose. I dismissed a star player immediately for poor attitude, attendance issues and theft. I got a lot of complaints from his parents. I had a very strict policy about having a thief on the team. He broke the rule and was removed from the team. We limped through another two-win season.

At the year-end banquet, I saw players that were happy to be a part of our team. They knew they had done it the right way and that our team stood for something. The wins and losses did not matter as much to them as knowing that they had been part of something that had meaning. I slept well that year and have every year since.

"My team is on the floor" - Gene Hackman in Hoosiers.

* * *

More areas to consider.

Grind it out - If we really enjoy coaching and assisting our players, we must persevere and work through the tough spots. Coaching is not easy and there are difficult challenges, but the rewards are tremendous. Those rewards may not be winning a championship, but they may be helping a player believe in themselves and accomplish something seemingly impossible.

Daily routine - Stability is very important during times of stress. Having a routine you can count on each day provides that rock in your professional and family life.

Fitness/nutrition - Including a fitness routine for at least every other day for 20 minutes or more, will help relieve stress. Use it to improve your health, and release some of the pressures of the job. Hectic schedules put you in a vulnerable position with respect to eating right. Do your best to make good choices when possible.

Genuine support - Having a mentor or someone in your family to share your thoughts with can reaffirm your love of the game and your players. Be willing to talk with those you trust about your situation.

Coaches typically feel more pressure from themselves to succeed than from any other source. We're driven, internally, to prepare our team to succeed through practice to every contest. When that breaks down, outside factors start to impact us and our team.

Recognizing those factors for what they are, and ultimately the fact that they have little to no power over you doing your job, will help. You were hired to coach and lead your team. Expectations may vary depending on where you coach and what your boss requires of you. But you have control over how you respond or act and how your team responds or acts to outside pressures. It serves no purpose to feed the fires of those who are not in your program. Only deal with what you *can* control and take care of your responsibilities in a professional manner.

Succeeding is more than winning games. Lay your head on that pillow and know you're on the right track.

28. Coaching Success, What's Your Definition?

I believe there's at least one point in any coach's career when they are mistakenly consumed with the idea that they're the true reason for their team's success. Leadership is a huge component of success, but a mediocre leader with talent may have a better chance of success than a great leader with no talent. Later, we'll talk about how you define success.

Don't get too sold on yourself

We were hot, winning a record 15 games in a row heading to the last week of the season. Our players had a combination of speed, skill, and unmatched determination. Confidence was overflowing. There were two tough games ahead against highly ranked opponents, and there was talk by our fans of an undefeated season. We were ranked in the top ten, and sports anchors were interviewing our players. This was clearly uncharted waters for an outstanding team. It was too much to handle as we lost the next two games with less than sterling performances. As a coaching staff, we knew we had to regroup and rebuild the confidence of our team for the tournament. For this group it was an easy task because they never stopped believing in what they could do. We would win the District, Region, Sub-Sectional and miss out on going to the Final Four by a heartbreaking goal in a 1-0 loss where we had many opportunities. I don't believe, before the season began, anyone expected this team to be so successful on the field. It had so much to do with their ability, attitude and what they wanted to accomplish as a group.

But, it wouldn't keep me from falling into that coaching trap with respect to *my* ability, although not for long. After all, we were losing nine talented seniors.

Talent wins games

We've all witnessed strong programs that simply continue to win regardless of who the coach is. The system and talent are in place year after year. We've also seen highly successful coaches take on struggling programs and get mediocre performances.

Let's never use 'lack of talent' as an excuse for not being successful. Coach the players in front of you with the same passion and determination, year after year, to the best of your ability. If you wait on that "star player" to move in, or that great group of young players to move up, you're cheating your current team and yourself. Many coaches will tell you they had their greatest years when they seemed to have less talent and lower expectations.

I once heard, "Yes, you're the leader and conductor of the team, but it's the beautiful music of highly skilled musicians that the audience hears during the performance. Without that skill there would be no concerto regardless of who the conductor was." (Source unknown.)

Talent wins games; coaches win strategy.

Keep building your vision every day

The reality is that coaches do their best work in the years before they break through with success. During that time, they work diligently every day, leaving nothing to chance, and they prepare their team for not only that season but the seasons to come. They have a vision that no one else can see.

Those seasons can be extremely stressful with pressure from administrators, parents (and even themselves) as they become restless and impatient for success. However, the results of all that work pay off.

Working with an inexperienced team or a team riddled with injuries forces coaches to use every resource they have to adjust and adapt at every practice and every game. That's where coaching is learned, through experience. Coaching highly skilled teams is rewarding, but pure coaching is making adjustments and decisions based on utilizing every advantage imaginable, even when there are none. Plus, seeing those teams reach success is the greatest feeling in the world.

Quote signed by the team given to me from the previous year in a huge upset win!

"There's no thrill in easy sailing when the skies are clear and blue, there's no joy in merely doing things which anyone can do. But there is some satisfaction that is mighty sweet to take, when you reach a destination that you thought you'd never make." Spirella

How will you define success?

As a coach, you have to answer the question, "What is success?" There are many different answers depending on your beliefs, values, priorities, etc. It may be wins, championships, titles, awards, accolades, rankings, star players, or something else. Regardless of the answer, it will always be your motivation for coming to work every day and the driving force behind your decisions. Once you have the answer, you'll be able to lead and guide your team and yourself toward that goal.

The journey is truly the greatest reward…

* * *

Here is a great example as told by Kevin Wright, Head Coach 2016 State Champion West Jessamine Girls Soccer and 2016 NSCAA KY Coach of the Year.

The West Jessamine Colts – aka, War Horses – started their quest to be the best in 2016. A storied program since 1997 had done everything except win a state championship. The team's theme and battle cry was "United West" and play as a "Wolfpack". Total team unity all in with a "Y'all Win Sisterhood Mentality." Five seniors, two commitments to play at the University of Kentucky, and a bunch of talented soldiers set their sights on a championship ring.

All seasons will come with a high price to pay and adversity. All smooth sailing produces a poor sailor. Before the season started one of our players, a highly touted freshman went on a mission trip to Haiti. Through her service for Jesus Christ and helping others, she acquired a bad case of four strands of E. coli. After making it home, she was confined to the hospital twice while battling her illness, but with the help, love, and prayers of family, teammates, friends and doctors she would pull through.

After six weeks, she was determined to return to the game she loved. Her will and fight inspired our whole team as we entered the state playoffs. Being ranked #4 much was expected, but rankings pale in comparison to the power of a teammate's inspiration.

We won the championship in the toughest possible avenue. Our bracket was loaded with both teams ranked above us, but we defeated both. One on a goal in the last minutes of the game and the other in penalty kicks. Our freshman goalkeeper was a phenom throughout the tournament and a staunch defense (that only allowed one goal in the last seven games) stepped up when needed. This team which scored 101 goals would not be denied.

* * *

The extrinsic rewards of being successful are great. It's a way to validate you and your team's hard work toward a goal of winning a championship. Those are wonderful memories for that team. What about that season or seasons when you weren't as successful? What will those players have to hang on to? I love winning just as much as any coach, but a trophy, no matter how large, will mean very little to anyone else and will gather dust in a trophy case. The journey you take each team on year after year, with each practice, game, and event will have the most impact on who they become.

Winning will always be the standard by which coaches are judged by spectators. Fair or not, that's reality. However, you'll be judged *by your players* for the rest of their lives in your approach, demeanor, and how you treated them while they were on your team. Success in this case surely means more than what is on the scoreboard. Through games, practice, travel and special events, you've shaped their lives and put them in situations allowing them to become stronger responsible adults. It isn't always peaches and cream, but neither is life. As people reminisce about their playing days later in life, hopefully a little smile will come across their face, and they'll appreciate what you did. To me, that's success!

29. Tracking Your Team without the Wins and Losses

How can you measure your team's progress without figuring in wins and losses?

Certainly wins and losses are how most people look at your team. But is that fair?

It takes extra effort to find a different measuring tool, but isn't 'going beyond the basics' what you ask of your team? You may not think you have the time or resources, but building a program requires you to measure and chart your team's progress in order to adjust your plans when necessary. Realizing you're on the right path or wrong path is a necessity. Somehow, you have to make it happen.

Where can you find the resources?

I know some teams have several student managers charting different indicators of success for players during practice and games. You may not have that luxury. How about parents? They love to video their sons and daughters? Why couldn't they chart specific skills during the game? In our example of soccer skills, these could include: Quality crosses in the box, Number of passes, Quality runs forward, Switching the field, Dropping the ball back, Shutting down an opposing player, Saves, Assists, Shots on Goal, etc. You can determine the measures based on position, importance, performance, or outcome with respect to your sport.

If you have more than one assistant coach, delegate some of the charting to them. Often during games, assistant coaches may not have specific duties other than to make recommendations about the game. Make use of their experience and knowledge. It's always nice if a former player volunteers, and certainly they can help as well.

Ranking your players

Measuring your team may be pretty easy with respect to how the top players have progressed, and how the bottom players have not. If I asked you to rank your players right now, could you do it? I'm guessing you'll say yes. As a coach, it's pretty easy to rank the top 3 or 4 players and the bottom 3 or 4 players. But what separates the middle players, your largest group? This group may be the key to your team reaching its goals. What goals have you set for this group? You know your top players need to be challenged every day and your bottom players need skill work and repetition. What do your middle players need? Do you know? Is their progress obscured by the demands you place on training your top and bottom players?

How can you begin to measure your players' progress?

Goal setting (soccer example addressed to each player)

We must have a destination, something to accomplish in soccer (by way of example) to gain confidence and become successful as the season progresses – both as an individual and a team. What those achievements or goals are is up to us, but without a map we won't arrive.

As you decide on your goals as an individual, remember it's good to aspire for greatness as an individual in a team sport. Through your personal commitment and sacrifice to achieve your goals, you'll improve your team and inspire teammates to become better. You simply won't settle for second best!

Goals can be simple to come up with, such as goals scored, saves, assists, etc., but what if you're an outside midfielder whose main focus is not scoring goals. What personal soccer goals could you come up with? What about:

1. Winning the ball back in three passes or less when the opposition steals the ball.
2. Making 12 quality runs to the touchline every game.
3. Replacing the defender on your side four times every game when they overlap.
4. Delivering six crosses into the box each game.
5. Switching the field or dropping the ball back five times a game.

Remember, goals must be specific, attainable and measurable.

Simply saying I'm going to play better tonight, I'm going to score more goals this year, I'm going to hustle more this year, isn't realistic. Players who have those goals are letting themselves off the hook, and not pushing themselves to their full potential. It's the easy way out, and more often than not will end up in frustration.

Have your parents, a friend, or someone on the bench record your efforts each game, and evaluate your progress. Your goals may be too high, or may need adjusting upward. Goal setting is a continuous process for the hungry player who wants to improve themselves and their team. Ask a coach if you need assistance in coming up with several goals.

In groups of three [each group should be diverse with respect to positions], come up with four specific goals for:

1. Strikers

2. Defenders (Outside and Central). Some goals may be the same.

3. Goalkeepers

4. Midfielders (Outside and Central). Some goals may be the same.

*Remember these can be practice and/or game related.

At our next meeting, we'll discuss all the goals listed, decide which ones meet our criteria, what it takes to achieve them, and you'll be asked to list your four for the season. After reviewing them, as a staff, we'll sit down with each of you and discuss your goals so that we all agree on your best path for success.

Next week our topic is "Team Goals".

Start thinking about our team goals; what we're committed to accomplish together. What we're willing to sacrifice to make it a reality, and how we'll get there. Being specific and settling for nothing less is the key. In our groups, we'll come up with the goals we can all agree on.

Here are some examples of team goals. They're not inclusive of every idea. Be creative and discuss what you want our team to accomplish. Keep in mind that goals have no substance without dedication and commitment to make them a reality. The foundation must be laid by every player doing their part, while encouraging and holding others accountable to doing theirs.

Goals are words that long to live and breathe; giving them life through your determination.

Team goals (soccer example)

1. 10 quality crosses in the box
2. 10 winning the ball back in 4 passes or less
3. 10 quality runs on the back post
4. 8 corner kicks
5. 10 switching the field
6. 10 shots on goal
7. 8 shots on frame
8. 100 % organization at the back; pressure, cover and balance.
9. A district championship
10. The regional championship
11. Win the state championship
12. Represent our school and family with dignity and integrity.
13. Encourage and support teammates at all times.
14. Play every game like it's the state championship
15. Practice every day with the same intensity and passion as a game.
16. Respect every opponent

As always, I appreciate your commitment, dedication, and effort for our team.

Coach _____

* * *

Coach Bob Koski, Head Varsity Track & Field Coach at Pojoaque Valley High School, Santa Fe, NM, who's coached 33 New Mexico State Track & Field Champions, (individual and relay), reminds us why goals are so important, and why our players must answer necessary questions in the goal-setting process.

The topic of setting goals is as talked about as training itself. Setting goals is a great way to help keep athletes motivated throughout the year. Goals need to be implemented not only during the competitive season but also during the off-season. Without goals, there is no direction. Goals should be set individually and as a team. Every team, coach, and athlete should have some sort of objective that they would like to accomplish during the season. Most of the time it involves making it into the post-season or winning a district or state title. Before you set a goal of this importance, think about what you will have to do to achieve it. Next, ask yourself the following questions:

1. Is my goal specific?
2. What is the timeline?
3. Can my goal be measured?
4. Is my goal attainable or realistic?
5. Is my goal relevant to the overall progress of the team?

* * *

Every player on your team needs specific goals to achieve, and a map to get there. It's your job to provide the leadership necessary to attain those goals. When players are asked to formulate goals for themselves, it creates a personal responsibility and accountability for them to accomplish. Guiding your players will allow them to grow and feel they did it by themselves. That should be your goal!

National Volleyball Coach of the Year Jean Kesterson reminds us of the "Characteristics of a Winning Team/Program" built through individual and team expectations.

- Coachable
- Complementary skills
- Empowering others
- Inspiring vision
- Intelligent individuals
- Mutual trust
- One mind working together
- Rewards
- Shared vision
- Take risks

* * *

30. Eight Questions That Keep Coaches Awake at Night

We rarely talk about the challenges of coaching that get locked inside (such as the ones listed below) and how to deal with them. We just think they are part of the job, feel we have all the answers, and often don't want to burden others with what can slowly extinguish our coaching passion.

Coaching is, after all, about the players, not us, and rightfully so.

But a release, or someone to share our thoughts with, can prove highly beneficial. Often assistant coaches are helpful here.

Nothing we face is so tough that we can't deal with it in a positive way. Of course, knowing that doesn't keep us from constantly asking bothersome questions!

1. Is it me? After a tough loss, or an unsuccessful season, it's natural to look in the mirror and ask yourself, "Am I the reason we aren't getting it done?" There are times when fans, parents, and even players let us know how terrible a job they think we're doing. On top of that, we're naturally hard on ourselves, having poured our hearts and souls into our teams and programs. So it's easy to let a thread of doubt creep in when our team comes up short of its capabilities. It's a common thought and, honestly, makes us work harder to improve.

Never stop believing in your ability, and continue to work toward becoming a better coach each day. For all the detractors, there are many more who believe in you. Continue to be strong.

"If you hear a voice within you say 'you cannot paint,' then by all means paint, and that voice will be silenced." Vincent Van Gogh

2. Why can't we reach that next level? When your team consistently reaches a certain level in the playoffs and can't seem to move on year after year, it's easy to start questioning your ability. There may be many reasons for this to happen, but it's likely that, before you arrived, your team hadn't reached its current level. You just have to be persistent and have a vision of where you want the team to go. Be relentless in working toward the goals you and your team established at the beginning of the season. Remember, there are no instant successes. Teams that continue to excel will gladly tell you how hard they worked and the challenges they overcame to be where they are today.

"If you don't shoot for the Stars, you'll never reach the Moon." Paul Davis

3. Is this the right team for me? There are top-tier teams, middle of the road teams, and bottom-tier teams. Which would you rather coach? Most would say top-tier teams. What some don't realize is that the majority of those top-tier teams are there because of the leadership of a special coach who had outstanding support and began their career with little experience. Certainly, talent plays a big part, but moving from team to team is not the answer. District, Region and Conference alignments often change, so moving to get away from a strong group of teams is not the answer. Five years is a good timetable for determining whether you can make a difference with a program. Your commitment is the key.

"There are only two options regarding commitment. You're either in or out. There is no such thing as life in-between." Pat Riley

4. How can I balance my personal life and coaching career? Ever give up a vacation or time with your family to coach your team? Were your family members upset, or did they support your decision? It's a tough position to put yourself and your family in. But, you were hired to coach the team and all the responsibilities that go with it, and coaching *will* interfere with personal plans. When you realize this going in, it makes it a little easier, but not always pleasant. Do your best to find and make time for your family; time that doesn't include anything to do with coaching or your sport. They will always be there for you and ultimately you may have to decide what your priorities are.

"Family is not an important thing, it's everything." Michael J. Fox

5. Did we really lose that game? There is nothing more gut-wrenching than waking up at 2 a.m. after a tough loss and, for a moment, trying to figure out if you won or lost the game. When reality strikes, it's very disheartening. How can you deal with that? Losing a big game is never easy. I always thought I had two choices: quit or be determined to do everything possible to help my team be successful.

Honestly, there were nights when quitting was the predominant thought. One night that desire to quit won out, and the next day I resigned. I felt I had let my team down and that it was better to step aside. I didn't even talk to my wife about it. Fortunately for me, my wife and some caring and level-headed players and parents weren't about to let that happen. I realized I had always told my players to never give up and now it was me who was giving up. After meeting with several of them, I understood I was just being selfish and only thinking of myself, so I came back. I will always be thankful to every one of them.

Never make a hasty decision based on emotion alone. Give it several days and talk with those whose opinions you value before making your decision.

"Tough times never last, but tough people do." Robert H. Schuller

6. What was my player thinking? When a player breaks a rule or expectation, and you have to sit them out or suspend them, it can put a dent in your spirit. It always seems to happen when you have a big game and the team needs everyone to play their best. As a coach, you can't escape taking it personally, and feeling let down when you're counting on an individual. But experienced coaches realize let downs will happen many times. It's part of coaching, and these are young people who need guidance and leadership. It's not your fault, and you can only hope the player (or players) learn a valuable lesson from the experience and realize how much of what they do impacts others.

Players will very often make mistakes on and off the field – that's a given – it is how we react and respond which sets the tone for our relationship with those players. Always do what's best for the team regardless of who the player is.

"Discipline yourself and others won't need to." John Wooden

7. Why can't I enjoy a win longer? A coach once told me that wins are fleeting; just like the wind. They disappear in the night, and all that's left is the impression that it was just a game you were supposed to win. On the other hand, losses seem to haunt us for years and never leave our memory. Most coaches understand the need to celebrate a win on that day or night, but the next day brings new challenges to overcome. Other than winning a championship, enjoying a win is something you can't do for any extended period of time. In the coach's mind, winning is something we are supposed to do so it's hard to hang on to that good feeling for any period of time.

"You learn nothing from your successes except to think too much of yourself. It is from failure that all growth comes, provided you can recognize it, admit it, learn from it, rise above it, and then try it again." Dee Hock

8. Why do I do this? Often disruptions and challenges snowball and all hit at once. When this happens, it's easy to ask, "Why do I do this?" After some thought, the answer is simple: the players. They count on us day after day to be their leader and remain strong. It goes with the territory. Challenges presented by administrators, parents, players, and even ourselves and our family always will be there. Remember, if this career were easy, anyone could do it. You do it to make a difference in someone's life, and don't forget it. Yes, the hours are long, and the compensation is low, but the rewards of all those wonderful moments over the years make any challenge seem small. After all, you're working at one of the most wonderful jobs anyone could ever have.

**"It's not the load that breaks you down, it's the way you carry it."
Lou Holtz**

Through all the long days and nights of coaching that wear us down, there are shining moments each day – small and large – that allow us to see why we coach. Those sparkles, even on a bad day, are our players. They come to us full of anticipation, enthusiasm and boundless energy with dreams of playing a game with their teammates. It's our responsibility to put everything aside during that time and give them what they deserve: a positive, challenging and fulfilling experience with passion. We are their light, and that should never be taken for granted.

There are many challenges in coaching. Learning to deal with them is the key to your career. Keeping everything locked up inside and trying to be a tough man or woman is not the answer. Find an outlet, someone to talk to, or some other resource to help you through the tough times. A former coach or mentor is a great idea, or someone from completely outside the coaching profession. Remember, others have followed the same path you're on and can help.

A mentor of mine once told me, "What we do isn't measured in wins and losses. We're measured by the impact we have on the lives of our players long after they quit playing. Selfish interests will never see that." What a great philosophy.

31. Charisma.... Do you have it?

Have you been around, or watched, someone who you truly admire enter a room? The room grows silent in anticipation and respect for who they are; indeed, a tiny bit of fear surfaces with the knowledge that this person could engage you at any time! When the person speaks, the audience hangs on every word, and their delivery – with a certain charm – draws you in. You feel honored and know the speaker is talking directly to you. It's called Charisma.

What draws players and possible recruits to your team? Is it the school you represent with its deep heritage of winning? The possibility of playing or starting right away? Your facilities?

There are many schools that offer the above. So with the possibility of boosting your ego to new levels, I think you'd agree it has more to do with you. But wait, there are a lot of quality coaches. Why aren't other schools getting the best players also? There must be some personality traits that some coaches have or are more pronounced than others giving them an advantage. It's often called Charisma.

We often hear coaches speak phrases such as, "I'm tough on my players telling them what they *need* to hear, not what they necessarily *want* to hear", or "I'm demanding in practice pushing them to new levels they never knew existed" but this presents a paradox. How can they be that extreme and still retain quality players?

It's the balance between being an obsessive driver of talent and knowing how to relate to players in a real way that separates the great coaches from good coaches. Players know and will do anything for these coaches because they understand it's for their best interest, and they care about them.

Totally obsessed coaches only care about one thing… winning. They don't care who the players are as long as they do their job, and have no interest in any other aspect of their players' lives. These coaches usually are on the move from one school to another, and eventually drop out.

But what are the traits that give high-quality coaches their charisma?

Confidence - There is no wavering. They believe in everything they do. Just ask them.

Presence - Just watch them enter a room. It's like watching a movie star. You'll see it.

Interesting - They can talk about any subject, do it well, and convey information in an interesting way. People are drawn to them.

Make you feel important - They want to know everything about you, and continue to be interested in your life.

Responses - Totally frank. Never sugarcoated.

Vision/optimistic - Will gladly tell you where the program is headed and what they are going to accomplish.

Team first/uniting - Masters at bringing players together for a common cause.

Total honesty - They let players know at the beginning of the sacrifices they will have to make, and how tough it will be to accomplish success.

Knowledgeable - They are students of the game and know every aspect of it.

Thorough/detailed - Every practice and game is scripted and contingencies planned. Nothing is left to chance.

Okay, so if the above elements underpin charisma, the next question is whether charisma can be acquired. Whilst natural personality attributes are a good foundation, can it be learned and practiced? I believe it can. Experience can be our teacher; everyday situations can help us develop charisma.

Most of us turn charisma off and on depending on the situation. Children are continually trying to charm their parents or grandparents in an effort to get their way. Young people use it in an effort to impress someone they admire or whom they want to get to know better.

Coaches really turn it on when they're recruiting a top prospect. What we often forget is the fact that it can really be advantageous every day in building our program.

Remember charisma is making someone else (in this case our players, our boosters, parents, and anyone in our community) feel important and special about themselves and their ideas. Oddly, enough it's never really about us, nor should we make it; it's about who's in front of us.

Andrew Mehrtens, former New Zealand National Rugby Team and "All Blacks" player recalls a meeting with his Coach, Steve Hansen, which started with a team ditch-digging project, but soon turned to the importance of letting players know how much you believe in them.

[Hansen] *"What do you want to do in rugby? What are you looking forward to in the year? ... I'll back you, I'll crawl over broken glass for you."*

[Mehrtens] *I wasn't very assertive before then but the confidence he gave me was fantastic. Steve's strengths are clear: he is big on team culture and team environment; he is outstanding in breaking it all down to the simplest element of your game, clarifying what you have got to do, what you have got to focus on; he is voracious for knowledge and he has got heart. It might not look like it but he genuinely gives a damn about players, he wants to improve them as players and people. He really cares."* From "Steve Hansen's secret is simple: he cares" by Andrew Mehrtens, The Times, June 30, 2017.

So, here is what you can do to help build your charisma in everyday coaching situations with your players, a parent, or a booster in an effort to get a project started or considered.

When you meet:

No distractions - Put your phone away and minimize distractions. It sends a strong message to the person you're with that they have your complete attention.

Look them in the eye - Making eye contact projects many desirable traits, including warmth, honesty, sincerity, competence, confidence, and emotional stability.

Listen/Listen - When they talk, respond, not so much verbally, but non-verbally. Show interest. When you speak, don't offer solutions unless asked. When you do, in most cases you make the conversation about you, not them.

Highlight/Praise - No one receives enough praise. Tell them what they did well. Not only will they appreciate it, they'll appreciate that you noticed what they did. It will simply make them feel important.

Ask questions - An easy way to show someone that you're completely focused is to ask questions after he or she has spoken. For example, you could ask, "When you say _____, what do you mean?" It shows interest and individuals really enjoy reflecting on and answering questions.

Stay focused - If you're thinking about what you're going to say, you're obviously not fully listening to what they are saying. Stay engaged, patient and show sincere interest.

Pause before responding - When someone has spoken, see if you can let your expression react first, showing you're grasping what they've just said and giving their presentation or statements consideration.

Stay positive - The words you use impact the attitude of your audience and you. Everyone wants to be around optimistic, positive and happy people. The words you select can help others feel better about themselves, and make you feel better as well.

Be confident - Always admire the work of others. It shows that you don't have a big ego and you are confident in your own ability.

Believe your message - When you have something important to say, say it like you mean it. Be expressive. Speaking with conviction gains trust and belief. Show others the benefit to them for the ideas you have.

Develop a caring personality - A warm personality opens many doors. You must be honest, kind and just as importantly, empathetic of other people's struggles and achievements. Use heartfelt stories when appropriate.

Be yourself - If you watch a charismatic person, everything seems to flow naturally. Building charisma is all about being able to attract people to you, so your main focus should be to improve on the characteristics you already have, and to ameliorate your weaknesses.

32. Controlling Your Destiny

Coaching has so many dynamics. Some we can control, while others are out of our reach.

Want to have a long, illustrious career? Then only be concerned with what you can control. The keys below will help keep you on track and allow you to live your dream. The journey with the players, parents, officials and assistant coaches is one you wouldn't trade for any trophy.

Here are my keys to a long and rewarding career

Keep the Ego in Check - Remember it's not about you anymore, it's about your players and your team. It's not how much you know and boast about; it's how you act and represent your team. Lose the "I know more than you" attitude, exhibit humility, and appreciation. Showing you're human and that you can make mistakes (and deal with them) will carry you much farther than any other attitude.

Look Professional - You represent your school, your family, and your team. Think of them when you get ready for a game or practice. Your appearance speaks volumes about your respect for the game and your team.

Be Prepared - That means being properly ready for practice, games, scheduling, and travel. Leave nothing to chance. Taking care of every aspect beforehand allows you to be relaxed and creative and to concentrate on other challenges.

Keep a Calm Demeanor - Regardless of the situation, be the one in control of your emotions. Becoming enraged or upset will hinder your ability to make sound decisions at crucial times. Be especially cautious after games when you're upset because the team didn't play well.

Represent Your Team - Attend every meeting that relates to player recognition, such as all-state and all-region, where coaches vote. If you're not there, you're letting your players down.

Take the Blame and Give the Credit - After a loss, take the blame in front of the team and the media. After a win, give all the credit to your team. Players and teams know when they didn't play well. You can take care of the details at practice. Never call a specific player out in front of the team during the game or afterward.

Outwork Your Team - Work every hour possible for the team and the program. Long hours are part of the profession, whether it's reviewing film, planning practice, scheduling, or working on the field. If your team is selling a product to raise money, you need to do it as well. We expect our players to work hard, so we have to do the same.

Learn Every Day - Search every source possible for new material, new ideas to help you become a better coach. We spend a lot of time searching for technique and tactics, but often forget to spend an equal amount of time researching leadership and team building.

Trust your Team - Teach your players every day at practice, and then trust their decisions on the field, or on the floor, during the game. You learned to coach through the experience of seeing what worked and what didn't. They will do the same when you show encouragement and confidence in everything they do.

Be Quiet - Knowledge is power, so don't feel like you have to use it to disarm someone, whether it's a player, parent or another coach. Develop your listening skills and acknowledge other ideas.

Delegate - Use your staff in the best way possible. They want to contribute and are an integral part of the team's success, so give them specific duties at every practice and game. Doing this frees you up to take care of other areas.

Don't Feel You Have to Win Every Battle - Whether it's a player or parent who offers suggestions or complaints, don't feel you have to win every battle. Acknowledge what they have to say and explain your point of view in a calm, professional way. They may not agree with you, and it's not earth-shattering if you don't win that battle.

* * *

Coach Jody Hamilton, Head Baseball Coach at West Jessamine High, National Coach of the Year, and two time State Champion, offers insight on a battle many coaches face.

Do I talk playing time with parents?

I believe a large percentage of parents' complaints are initiated from their child's playing time or lack thereof. During 35 years of coaching four different high school sports and holding the position of Athletic Director, discussing a player's playing time was once considered a non-issue and parents accepted this decision. But in the last few years, parents have become increasingly and extremely vocal, breaking down the bond of coach/player relationships.

In the past, the profession of coaching was perceived differently by parents and student-athletes.

- Coaching decisions were made by the coach; parents wouldn't ask questions because of the chance of embarrassment to the child.

There are concerns to all when meeting with parents and discussing playing time.

- The coach and player might both be put in a tough situation. Respect and Trust could be lost or damaged.

- Coaches might feel their integrity or knowledge is being questioned.

- A message might be sent to all. If Johnny plays then there will be a line at the door of parents expecting the same. If Johnny doesn't play, the parent feels that the coach holds a grudge and doesn't like his/her child or is unapproachable.

- If he plays, other players will assume it's only because his parents complained, begged, bribed or threatened the coach.

This year I opened the door to all parents who had concerns about playing time. It eliminated a large number, but not all, of the complaints.

There are some ground rules that need to be established before any conversation can take place.

- The player needs to be present or have knowledge of the meeting.

- There can be no discussion of other teammates.

- There needs to be a neutral person at the meeting such as Athletic Director, Trainer, or Principal.

- Let parents know that final playing time decisions will be made by the coaching staff.

I believe Tommy Lasorda says it best, "I motivate players through communication, being honest with them, having them respect and appreciate your ability and your help."

* * *

Feed Your Passion - Attend every clinic, convention, residential course, and seminar possible. Get the school or booster organization to pay for all or part of the costs when you can. Learning new concepts from the elite in your profession will inspire you to reach new heights.

Take Time for Yourself and Family - Your family and your health should be of most concern. Take time away from your job to relax and enjoy being with your family. You will never be able to relive moments taken away by your career, and without your health you won't be able to do your job. Keep your priorities in balance.

Embrace Your Players - Players need to know you care about them. Find out all you can about their hobbies and interests. I highly recommend having a talent show night for your team. You will be amazed at the talent they possess away from the field! When you show a genuine interest in their lives, they're willing to work harder for the benefit of the team.

Recognize Your Assistants - Being an assistant coach is the purest form of coaching. Assistants don't have to worry about the issues and paperwork that come with being the head coach. However, sometimes they aren't recognized at the district, regional or national level like head coaches. So go overboard and recognize them in the local media and at the banquet.

Communicate and Cooperate - Develop a good relationship with the booster or parent organization. They work hard behind the scenes for the benefit of their children and the team. Pitch in and help at any time possible; it will earn you bonus points. Work with your AD in a positive manner. When he or she helps your team, let them know how happy you are and thankful for their efforts.

It's easy to get caught up in the day-to-day responsibilities of coaching. However, by keeping the ideals outlined here in sight, you can serve in a way that will enhance everyone's experiences and keep that coaching fire burning bright. That's what coaching is all about.

33. Working with the Athletic Director

Have you ever thought about what it takes to be successful as a coach? If your Athletic Director asked what you needed from him or her, what would you say? And how would you rank your list?

Family - *Allow me time to spend with my family.*

The support and encouragement you receive from your family are so important. Balancing time and energy between those you care for most, and your vocation, is essential. There will be times when coaching will require most of your time. Having an understanding family and finding a way to budget your limited time is a challenge. The phrase "married to your job" should never be taken as a compliment. If your family situation is in disarray due to your job, then it's impossible to focus on your team. Time spent with your family is always more important than the time immersed in your job. Our schools need to do more to bring our coaching families together, such as recognizing and celebrating them with picnics and outings.

Players - *I need players who are competitive and have a passion every day.*

We all want the best players available but will that guarantee our success? No, but it's a start. There will be seasons when you'll have more role players than stars, and other years when it will be reversed. It's always going to be our job to mold them into a team, develop their individual skills, feed their competitive hunger and lead them toward success. How do you get those players? Be a salesperson. Talk to everyone you meet about your passion for the job, your school and the vision of success you see. It all begins with your competitiveness and passion for the game.

Facilities - *Let me be a voice in the vision for our facilities.*

Will a first-class arena, stadium or training facility bring us a title? Maybe not, but it just might. Having the best may bring new players and their families to your school. It may also bring playoff games to your school and the chance of playing a tournament game at home. While facilities may be out of your control, you can still have influence on upgrades or the planning of a new complex. Press your AD, administrators, board members and parents for better facilities and let them know how it will benefit the players and the school. Schools listen to parents with a cause. Use their determination to better your program.

Compensation - *Work to keep my salary current and fair.*

All of us want to be fairly compensated for our work, but the majority would say the time we put in is more than any of us can be compensated for. Salary is certainly important with respect to taking care of ourselves and our families, but I believe we'd work for less, if we had to, because of our love for our sports and the challenges we face every day. Check other coaches' salaries who are in comparable situations. Always stand up for what you believe to be fair for the work you're doing.

Resources/funding - *Provide the budget to equip a first-class team.*

Equipping our teams with the best uniforms, training equipment, etc. and having the budget to take them away to camp or games that require extended stays can make a difference to the success of a team. Always be willing to challenge your AD when you think the budget is unfair for what your team needs. If you never ask for it, you can be assured you won't get it.

Acknowledgement - *Appreciate the job our team is doing.*

We all need to be appreciated in our profession. It doesn't mean we have to be Coach of the Year, just an acknowledgment every once in a while with a pat on the back or kind word letting us know someone sees and understands our hard work and effort. While we have little control over this, it feeds our passion and love for the game and what we're doing. We can only hope we work for someone who understands what it takes to coach a team through challenges and jubilation.

Communication - *Be clear in your coaching expectations.*

Having an AD who is clear with respect to coaching expectations, who keeps you informed on rule changes, the paperwork required, player eligibility, field maintenance challenges, and so on, can mean so much. A great AD will keep you from being blindsided by obstacles that may impact your team. Let them know how much you appreciate all they do. Visit and talk with them regularly, even when you don't need something. Their first thought when they see you coming shouldn't be, "I wonder what he or she wants now!"

Consistent decisions - *Show strength and conviction in your decisions.*

Just as our players expect us to be consistent in our decisions, we expect our boss to do the same. Being able to count on those decisions during times of crisis, or even knowing they're going to discipline us if we get out of line, is important. Every decision they make in regard to our team may impact the chance we have to reach our goals. I feel certain we all want to work for someone who's strong in their conviction for all the sports programs, and isn't afraid to make a tough decision.

Evaluation - *Make me a better coach.*

Without being evaluated, how will you ever know what areas you are strong in, and which areas need improvement? This can be an uncomfortable situation for some coaches. I think most of us know the areas we're strong in, but it's nice to hear someone else agree with our perception. Areas of concern may be tricky, but let's face it, we all have things we can become better at. Embrace the fact that someone is working with you in an effort to make you a better coach. Honestly, if we aren't evaluated, we feel slighted and insignificant.

Take the time to meet with your Athletic Director and map out a plan for your success. We spend a lot of time developing practice plans, game schedules, player evaluations, etc. and often have very little time thinking about the priorities that impact our ability to coach effectively. Our Athletic Director, besides being our boss, is a great resource to assist us every day. Take advantage of their experience and knowledge at every opportunity.

What is your Athletic Director looking for as they evaluate and assess your performance and day to day impact?

* * *

Daniel Sandlin, former Athletic Director at East Jessamine High School, lists several expectations that Athletic Directors look at in a coach's performance.

High-Level Communicator - Coaches that communicate effectively with players, parents, and the community. Also, a coach that will be able to share his or her vision with all involved.

Involved in the community - A coach that is willing to get into the community in their sport's area and offer camps. Plus we want a coach that is involved in their players' lives in the community. Overall we are looking to better the community through the school.

The Vision for the Program - In all programs, you need a vision on where you stand and where you plan to go. Within that vision, you need to know who is on board and who is going to drive the ship.

Practices with a purpose - Coaches each day go to practice, but are they working on skills or situations for the betterment of the team and the individual player? For example, if you had a team in basketball that is having trouble breaking the press you would make sure the next day's practice is specific to that need.

Accountability for assistant coaches and players - Head coaches need to hold themselves to a high standard as well as their players and assistant coaches. We cannot expect players to come to practice each day ready to work if we are not doing the same as coaches. Head coaches need to realize they are only as good as their assistant coaches.

Character and High Energy - We want a coach that comes to every practice, meeting session, training session, and game, with tons of energy because everyone feeds off of that energy. However, that coach needs to do that with the highest character to make sure that he or she is teaching his players the proper way to communicate, act, and work each day.

Organized and Structured - When you go to a practice, it should be a finely-oiled machine with each player improving because the practice is well planned. For a head coach, you need to make sure that your players and coaches can go to work each day with the least number of problems. Being organized does not mean you have a neat desk, it means you have a plan and you know how that plan is going to be carried out each day. Structured programs have rules and everyone has to follow those rules. No one person is bigger than the program.

Challenges every athlete - I want a coach that when their players leave practice every day they believe they have gotten better in some area. Each player needs to elevate their game each day through hard work and practice. From the bottom player to the top we want them to work and improve.

Creates a positive relationship with all players - Coaches need to know where their players come from each day. The coach needs to be the person that their players trust each day. As a coach, you need to know as much as possible about your players to be able to relate to them and know how to make them become better players and people.

Standards of excellence cannot be compromised - If you set a standard as a coach, you cannot go back on that. If someone is dragging the group down, you have to move on if they no longer want to work towards that standard. Athletes will only work as much as you make, or challenge, them to each day.

Has a process that leads to success - Many coaches have a plan, but they don't know how to carry it out. The details of that plan are essential. A coach must be able to lead their players to success in their sport and in life, then continue to put that process into every area of their program.

Supports his or her athletes in other sports - In high school, you need to have athletes playing more than one sport to be able to have good programs. Plus college coaches have said several times that they like to recruit players that play more than one sport in high school. With those two statements, a player has to feel that his coach supports him to play another sport. As a coach, you need to make sure that your players know you want them to play other sports and they want to see their coaches at their games.

* * *

34. Officials, Do You Have Their Respect?

Do you plan everything possible to control the game, giving your team the best opportunity to succeed? I feel certain the answer is yes, but what is your relationship with officials like?

Do you greet them? Avoid them? Ever wonder what your reputation is in the officials' community? Should you care or be concerned?

Most of us would justify the confrontation of officials as a way of supporting and fighting for what is right for our teams, but does such behavior help or hurt our cause? Honestly, have you ever seen an official reverse a call in one of your games? While you may believe your pleas and remarks are setting up the next call, do such actions really work in your favor?

In one of our basketball games, a ball hit off two or three players simultaneously and went out of bounds. I clearly had a view of the last player to touch the ball, and it was our opponent. In a rush to make a call, the official, who had gotten turned around, didn't see who touched the ball last. He signaled that it was our opponent's ball. I was livid and yelled to no avail. On the next play, close to our bench as he handed the ball to our player, I quietly asked him, "Did you see who last touched the previous ball?" He confidently answered, "Coach, I was out of position, did I get it right?"

I was astounded. Was I hearing him correctly? To my surprise, suddenly I was okay with the play. He admitted he made a mistake, just like I do when I coach. My respect for him would continue to grow throughout our careers. All you can ask is for officials to be honest and to do their best in any situation.

How can you build respect and rapport with officials?

Meet and greet every official at every game - Shake their hands, let them know you're glad to see them, and set the tone for a great game. If anything to do with your roster or facilities needs mentioning, make them aware.

If it's a home game, make sure your field or court is in order - Your facilities are a reflection of you, your team and your school. Whether it's under your supervision or not, do everything to make it first class and ready to go. If officials need to dress at your facility, make the dressing room the best one they will ever use.

Avoid objections on every call - Screaming and yelling all night long will only lessen your effectiveness when that one big call goes against your team. If they've heard you all night long, why should they take you more seriously in this situation? Save it, and only yell when necessary.

Stick to the call, avoid being personal - When you do yell over a call, do your best to keep the rhetoric contained to the particulars of the call. Once it goes personal, you stand the chance of getting a yellow card, technical foul or even thrown out of the game. Being tossed out rarely helps your team.

Have your team properly equipped - When your team takes to the floor or field, have them ready to go. Make certain they're properly equipped according to the rules of your game. It can be a huge distraction to a player when an official asks them to remove something before a game.

Look them in the eye and let them know you need them to have the best game they've ever had - Have the courage to ask them something you ask your team every night you play, "I need for you to have the best game you've ever had."

Have control of your team - Officials know from previous games or other officials if your team is uncontrollable. When this happens, they will inadvertently look at your team for all fouls in most situations. Take care of this when you build the culture of your team.

Learn from them - Great officials teach the game as well as officiate it. We have one official in our area who teaches our JV players as he calls the game. Why not. He's helping our players understand the rules. Most confident officials will explain a call to you if you have an objection.

Thank them after every game - Win or lose, shake their hands after every game. Even if your team had its worst game, and they missed some calls, find the strength to be a bigger man or woman and thank them for the job they do.

I've had incidents where officials stopped the game and asked me to address an unruly crowd, required our players to cut their fingernails, made our players remove piercings, and even baited our players by asking them to remove hairpins during warm-ups, before stopping the game immediately after kickoff to see if they had.

Ironically, all these incidents were on the road with the exception of the unruly crowd. Building rapport is easier at home games because you often see the same officials time and time again. However, when you take your team on the road, you have to start all over again at earning respect.

Naturally, my players were visibly shaken at these incidents, not understanding why they were being singled out. In most cases, it was the rules the officials were enforcing. Remember, it's our job as coaches to make sure our teams are properly equipped, so this was on me. We can also prepare our teams to understand that rule interpretations and enforcement may vary, and they should not be surprised or upset if asked to make adjustments.

Officials have a job to do, just as we do as coaches. The key is to lay the groundwork for a professional relationship with every official, based on you and your team's words and actions. Without officials, our sports would just be chaos. When you treat them with respect, you've created an atmosphere that gives your team the best chance to succeed.

35. Assistant Coaches, What makes them so special?

I've worked with several coaches on my staff over the years, and it was always a rewarding experience. I will admit I'm not the best at delegating, so in that sense I probably didn't take advantage of every attribute they offered.

If you look for the purest form of coaching, you'll find assistant coaches. They can concentrate on working with players to play the game with respect to skill, technique, strategy, and more. There's nothing distracting them such as administrative duties, parental issues or discipline; these are usually taken care of by the head coach. But, they also have to be ready to assume head coaching responsibilities at any time.

What does it take to be a great assistant coach?

Loyalty - Always maintain your loyalty to the program and the coach. Others may try to manipulate you against the head coach. If you don't believe in the head coach and where the program is headed, voice your opinion to the coach. If nothing changes, don't compromise your beliefs, resign.

Support - Encourage your players at every opportunity. There may be times when the head coach needs to hear support from you as well.

Flexibility - Practice and game schedules change daily. You have to be flexible with respect to your work and family.

Opinions - If you and the coach always agree, one of you isn't necessary. Offer differing opinions that need to be heard.

Solutions - Be vocal about what you see at practice and the game, and what you feel will work.

Coaching - Be able to coach during practice and the game, in the absence of the head coach, or when called upon.

Dependable - Earn respect from the players and coaches by always being at practice and games.

Educate - Explore every resource available to improve your coaching education and what you can share with the team. Make yourself valuable. If your goal is to be a head coach, work on acquiring your coaching diplomas and licenses during this time.

Get dirty - Do the things no one wants to do. Lead by example and show how hard you're willing to work. Impressions mean everything.

Counselor - In many cases, players will come to you with issues and problems instead of the head coach. Listen and work with them to come up with solutions if possible.

Communicate - Approach the head coach when you have any idea about team building, practice, lineup, strategy, etc. There's a good chance he or she hasn't even thought of it.

Professional - You represent your family, your school, and the team. Act and look the part.

Step forward - Be willing to step up and let the coach know when you can handle an activity or situation. Showing your ability will give the head coach more confidence.

* * *

Coach Bob Koski, Head Varsity Track & Field Coach at Pojoaque Valley High School, shares his thoughts on why Assistant Coaches are vital to a team's success.

I feel the biggest attribute an assistant coach can have is being trustworthy. Can you trust them to execute the team's plan and philosophy? Can you depend on them to be there when needed? Do they make good choices with and for the athletes without constant direction? Managing a team with multiple assistant coaches is very similar to co-parenting and running a household. All responsible parties need to share "the load" of daily and weekly tasks as agreed upon. Everyone has a skill set of strengths and should be utilized accordingly. The use of "one voice" throughout the team should be the theme. Clearly, one of the reasons for our success on and off the track was a combination of many special qualities that assistant coaches brought to our program.

* * *

There's a good chance that any success your program has had over the years is due, in large part, to the work of your assistant coaches. A head coach simply can't do it all, even though some think they can. Assistant coaches are the lifeblood of a program. They continually work with the younger players on development and maturation. It is encouragement and motivation that allows these players to be ready when they move up.

How can you strengthen your assistant coaches?

Confidence - Every time you have the opportunity, let them know through your words and actions that you have faith in what they do.

Coaching - You don't need someone to pick up equipment after practice, or other menial tasks. You need someone to coach your players. When the time is right, give assistant coaches the opportunity to take over practice and/or coach the varsity in a game, not just the younger team. This will free you up to spend more time evaluating players. Without experience, assistants will never grow.

Appreciation - Thank them every chance for all they do, whether on the field, in public, or at the banquet.

Delegate - Have specific tasks for them to accomplish with your team, especially early in their careers. As they grow, all you need to give them is a topic or area to focus on, and let them decide how best to teach it.

Professional - Always treat them as professionals. If you have any issues with something they've done or failed to do, talk with them away from the team and other coaches in a professional manner.

Expectations - Have standards for your coaches just as you do for your players. Coaches must always be held to a high standard of accountability.

Philosophy - Help them develop 'in progress' coaching philosophies, and explain why they need one.

Evaluate - Take the time to evaluate their performances for the year by highlighting areas of strength and areas that still need some attention.

Listen - Every time your coaches suggest something for practice, during a game, or any other time, give them your full uninterrupted attention. You may be inclined to jump into the conversation early, but let them finish. Rather than belittle anything they say, just repeat what they said with, "So if I understand correctly, you're saying_____, and fill in the blank with their statement. Let them hear it back before discussing the merits of the statement. Always make them feel comfortable making suggestions at any time.

Media - Give them the opportunity to talk with reporters after a game. It gives you a break from saying the same thing every night, and allows your assistants to learn and prepare for their head coaching careers.

Be patient - You started somewhere, and probably made a mistake or two. Have patience early in their careers and do your best to train them correctly. If they aren't making a mistake, they probably aren't doing anything.

I've always enjoyed sitting and watching as our staff coached and interacted with the younger players during their games. It was a little less stressful, and our coaches were always trying to look at new ways to make our players more successful. Even after a hard-fought loss, the coaches helped them feel a great sense of accomplishment.

Personally, I was an assistant for six years, for four different coaches, in three sports. Twice, I was a volunteer assistant laying the groundwork in an effort to get hired. It allowed me to grow as a coach and formulate ideas on how I would coach when given the opportunity. In two situations, my style and the head coaches' style were completely opposite which, at the time, bothered me. But, looking back, it was the perfect situation for the team and the ideas I could offer, even though personally I couldn't compromise my beliefs and principles.

I owe so much to the assistant coaches I've worked with. They've always treated our players with respect, and represented our program in a positive manner. I'm blessed and feel honored to have been associated with them. Through their tireless efforts, our players and programs always improved. Take the time to thank and recognize those you coach with; they need to know you care and appreciate what they do.

36. Challenges and rewards, part of the process

Have you ever put your heart and soul into reaching a goal or accomplishment? It can be challenging due to situations you've never encountered and little experience to draw from. Plus those who are in your group or team may not have the same motives, goals or determination. What happens when they start to complain and drop out on a journey you've dreamed about for years?

My wife and I have been avid hikers, with some of the highlights being in Colorado, hiking "14ers" as they're called (peaks that are 14,000 feet or higher). We reached the summit on Long's Peak and Gray's and Torres. Both were different climbs with varying challenges. After we reached the top in both, the sense of accomplishment was great, but, honestly, the views and experiences on the way up were the most rewarding thing.

As I look back, it's so similar to coaching. As you ascend on your coaching journey of building a program, the winds will howl and blow, storms will roll in, and your will and determination to keep going will be tested, by yourself and those around you.

Some of those challenges might be:

- Losses that linger, while victories seem to disappear.

- A parent confronts you after a win to complain about playing time.

- Your field is a mess and will only be ready when you put in extra time.

- A hateful email or text message tells you how terrible you are.

- Your best player isn't eligible for the next game because of grades.

- Your best prospective players end up playing for another team.

- The referee stops the game and threatens to end it unless you quieten unruly fans.

- An unsigned letter arrives in the mail. I think you know what it says.

- No one thanks you for a job well done because that's what's expected.

- Selfish parents and players confront you with self-serving issues.

- Long hours, late weeknights, weekends and very little family time.

- You must face those who are against you, sometimes even your players.

- A voicemail is left on your phone. It's not a compliment.

- An administrator confronts you about playing time for their child.

- All-Tournament Team selections create jealousy.

* * *

Cy Tucker, seven-time Kentucky Girls High School Soccer State Champion at South Oldham High School, and all-time winningest coach in Kentucky acknowledges a big challenge, and how coaches can deal with the demands every day.

It confounds me that there are a growing number of parents and players who would choose playing time over winning a state championship. That has become the biggest bump in the road in my opinion. The use of social media and the internet have become an easy and cowardly way to criticize coaches and often to larger audiences. Following our surprising 7th State Championship in 2014, there were parents glaring at me in anger!

The road to the coaching summit is indeed a rocky one. It has become more so in the last 13 years. I know of one high school coach who several years ago received death threats toward him and his family.

This places an even greater importance on coaches' resilience as they try to do what's best for the team. Coaches can find resources for resilience through developing relationships with other coaches. The sharing of experiences and strategies for dealing with challenges is very important. Feeling as if you are part of a community, rather than in exile, helps lessen the effect of the negativity that coaches can receive. I would encourage all coaches to join organizations and/or pursue contemporaries in order to have resilience resources available.

* * *

While these and many other challenges aren't new, and most of us expect issues to arise over a season or career, they should not take away from the wonderful experiences we encounter. That's what keeps us focused and motivated to continue building our program.

Some of the thrills you may experience are:

- The first day with your new team – a memory of a lifctime!
- Planning for practice, a proud sense of leadership.
- Teaching the game comes so easily because of your passion.
- Seeing players genuinely care for each other.
- Watching a player's reaction after an accomplishment. Priceless.
- A player thanks you for something you did.
- Attending clinics and seminars to expand your knowledge is fun.
- Talking with fellow coaches about trends and new ideas.
- Smelling the grass, seeing the crowd, warming up your team.
- Winning a game you weren't supposed to win.
- Your team being acknowledged by officials as being very respectful.
- Going to camp with your team!! Memories of a lifetime!
- Taking your team on a High Ropes Course!
- Seeing your players' other talents on talent night! So much fun!
- Sharing some life lessons before and/or after practice.
- That moment when players realize it's not all about them.
- Guiding players through difficult times in their lives.
- Learning to compromise over things that really don't matter.
- Picture day. Is this the same team?
- Senior Night, a special night for those who've been loyal. Emotional.
- Former players getting together on Alumni Night, the hugs and thanks.
- Seeing and talking with former players who are now coaching.

u deal with all the challenges?

,pe so because coaching is one of the most rewarding careers in the world. The joy of helping young people succeed, on and off the field, is something you can't put a price on. So much has nothing to do with technique, tactics, or conditioning but comes down to communication, caring, responsibility, understanding, and the ability to not be distracted by those who are not in your corner. We, as coaches, must always do what's best for our players, and as the games begin, what's best for our team.

Your ability to positively influence your players will always outweigh any negatives. Stay true to what you believe in, and keep on climbing. Just take a moment when the storms start to roll in and look out over the beautiful landscape, thinking about those who are counting on you and remember why you're on this journey.

37. Looking for that Coaching Passion? It May Be in a Camp

Are you mentally drained after a tough season? Do you find it a grind, in day-to-day operations, when building a program? If you pour your heart and soul into the job of coaching, you've been there (and probably quite often).

I'd like to offer an unconventional treatment for coach burnout: Camp.

Some of my greatest joys have been when conducting a camp, taking my team to camp, and everything else in between. In fact, I'd say one of the most rewarding aspects of coaching is conducting a camp. Seeing the eager faces of very young players who anticipate every word, and who show their enthusiasm for every activity, will bring back your energy and love for your sport.

Conducting a local summer youth camp

When setting up a camp of your own, there are several things to consider:

Location - Make it as accessible as possible for the maximum number of campers. Do you have a contingency plan in case of bad weather?

Insurance - I highly recommend taking out a one-time policy in case of injury or something unexpected. Are you covered at the location of the camp, or does your personal policy cover you? There are companies that specialize in camp insurance.

Expenses - What will the location cost? Staff? Brochures? Equipment? T-shirts? Prizes? Guest Speaker?

Camp theme - Why should your athletes come, and what will you emphasize?

Guest speaker - Will you have a special person to highlight in your brochure?

Prizes - Consider buying DVD's to give away in a raffle each day.

T-shirts and sport-relevant equipment - These are expected at camp.

Waiver - Have each camper's parent sign a waiver relieving you of responsibility in case of injury or accident. While this may make you feel safe, check with an attorney to see how safe you really are.

Advertise - Use social media, develop a camp webpage, use Twitter, involve the local newspaper, etc.

Cost - What will you charge your campers?

Profit - Camps are not big money makers if you're doing them for the kids. Most of your profit, if any, will go towards items for the players and your staff. Your main goal should be to spread a love and passion for the game, for the players to have fun, and to promote yourself and your program.

Daily schedule - Have everything planned out each day so the campers know the agenda.

Staff responsibilities - Make sure you have specific duties and responsibilities for your staff and they clearly know what they're doing. Assistant coaches and former players make great camp leaders. You may want to put one of them in charge so you can be free to oversee the camp.

Fun - Campers want to have fun and learn at camp. Emphasize the fun part. It should be a memory they cherish for the rest of their lives.

Team camps

Taking your team to a team camp in the off-season is a must! I did it practically every year. The benefits are many, and to see another side of your players is a special experience.

Choosing the right camp is a challenge, so consider:

Cost - The expense to send a child to a residential camp for a parent is a huge undertaking. Currently, camps run from $400-$550 in our area for a 3- or 4-day camp. Try to balance cost with benefits. You may want to consider a commuter camp to cut the cost in half, but what you lose by not staying is worth a whole lot more.

Camp - What does this camp offer? What are other coaches' opinions? There are some camps that may be disappointing. Do your research.

Teams - For team sports, what other teams (specifically) are registered? You want your team playing against the best competition possible, and it's also nice to play teams you won't see in the regular season.

Agenda - Look at the schedule and make sure the majority of time is planned for skill and team development. Outstanding camps include Leadership training, Team Building, Strength and Conditioning, and Nutrition sessions. Downtime for any extended period is not good for your team, and it's not what they paid for.

Staff - Who, specifically, will be training your team? If they don't meet with your approval, say so. Your team is paying to improve!

Size - Is the camp too big for your team? Some camps are all about volume, and your team may get lost in the shuffle, especially if they aren't one of the big-name teams attending.

These are team camp activities that really impressed me

Talent show - A tremendous idea on one night of the camp. The players get to choose their theme and produce a skit. You could have several scenarios and have them blindly draw three to choose from. It was awesome!

4 V 4 tournament - It's a Dutch tournament, mixing and matching players from all teams. Use a points system for the player or players who end up on the winning team the most. After each game, players are assigned to a different group. It's a great way for players to get to know each other.

Team building - Some camps use a session each day with fun team building games with a purpose. The players love them, and it's usually inside, out of the heat, which gives them a break. With technology, players can look up lyrics to a song and perform as a group.

Water Park - A camp we attended was close to a water park so they bused the players over for a couple of hours to relax.

World Cup - Each team is assigned a country. They get face paint, and make t-shirts for their team. At night with the fields lit up, the camp administrator leads all the teams into the stadium like they do at the Olympics. Teams play a 7 V 7 round robin tournament until the early hours of the next morning. It was a blast! Some teams even had players dressed as cheerleaders!

Some of the many benefits of a residential camp

1. Brings your team together
2. Competition
3. See players in a different setting
4. Challenging
5. Extra practice sessions/games

6. Allows you to evaluate players

7. Exposes them to new coaching techniques

8. Meet new friends

9. See players in new roles

10. Skill development

Going to team camp for us was always one of the highlights of the year. I must admit my disappointment with some camps. However, the ones that were great were led by a coach/administrator with enthusiasm and a passion for the game. You knew it when you shook his or her hand.

We had some special moments at camp and, honestly, if I asked my former players who won the game on a certain date, they would look at me like I was crazy and say how would I know that? But if I gave them a camp we attended and asked if they remembered the crazy talent show, or extravagant 7 V 7 Tournament we were in, they would remember in a second!

Take time to do the extra things that will make you and your team special. Conduct a camp in the summer to promote your great game, to help build your program, and by all means take your team to a residential camp. The benefits and memories will last a lifetime.

38. Five Ways to Establish Rapport with Officials

What's your relationship with game officials? Cordial, business-like, no relationship at all? Do you see officials as just part of the game? Do you wonder why you should make any effort to establish a professional relationship with someone who you might argue with? They have a job, you have a job, why bother? Maybe you think you have already established a reputation in the officiating community. Why should you care?

Let's agree that officials have great games, and games that are not their best. Can we help them have a better game? I believe we can. Our reputation sets the tone for them to feel comfortable coming into our stadium or arena, or if they show up at one of our road games. That positive tone impacts our game more than we realize.

Here are five ways to build a long-lasting positive relationship.

1. Greet officials before every game - Make a point to shake their hand, look them in the eye and say, "I really appreciate you being here tonight, and thanks for your dedication to all the players. Have a great game." You can vary the statement, but be sincere in what you say. Without officials, even on a bad night, our sports wouldn't exist.

2. Expect your players to be respectful - Show your players exactly what you expect when they meet and deal with officials. "I understand," "thank you," "I see," are all phrases that show respect when players communicate with officials. Remind your players that becoming upset with a call and yelling at the official will never help your team. Be firmly in control of your team with respect to, and the respect of, officials. Never tolerate anything less.

3. Keep coaching, not officiating - I've witnessed coaches become so upset with an official that they stopped doing actual coaching while the game went on, only to continue yelling and screaming. Their job is to coach. Pick a time during halftime, timeout, or stoppage to plead your case, then let it go. Rarely will a call be changed. Officials will miss calls just as we will make mistakes coaching. Take a deep breath and stay focused.

4. Recognize officials and their achievements - If you're fortunate to live in the same area, greet officials every chance you get. It's when you see them with their family that you realize they are more than just the shirt they wear during a game. Become involved in recognizing great officials and their dedication to the profession. Sell their ability just as you do your players. Call, email or message the head of officials in your area with a compliment. It may be one of only a few he or she receives.

5. Champion a Cause - We often associate with fellow coaches, but have you ever thought that officials might have the same passion to make a difference in a player's life as you do? Who better to team up with and lead the fight for a cause than officials? Getting to know each other better is certainly a benefit, but seeing the difference you both can make is very rewarding. It can even be played up in the press, such as "Who would have thought that Coach Wilson and Mark Press, lead official in the XYZ conference would see eye to eye on anything?" It makes a great headline and promotes your cause.

The people who are under as much pressure as you are the officials. If you think that having a parent(s) after you during, or after, a game is bad, just think about the officials. They have just about every fan on both sides at least once during a game, and usually a lot more, after them.

I've been blessed to have outstanding officials over my career. Getting to know most of them was a joy. They have families, challenges, hopes, and dreams, just like you.

Take the time today to genuinely meet and greet every official at your games. Getting to know someone who cares as much as you do about making a difference in our young players' lives is a memory you won't soon forget.

39. Will you remain loyal to a program you built?

During the off-season, have you ever considered applying for (or gauging interest in) another coaching opportunity? There's so much to consider. Why would you change? What does that program offer that you don't have at your current school?

Often coaches who've come off a challenging season start thinking it may be time to move on, or change. What factors drive that thought process? Here are a few:

- Wins were few and far between
- Injuries decimating the team
- Parents who were very challenging
- Very little talent coming back, the future looking bleak
- No support from the AD and other administrators
- Facilities continuing to deteriorate
- No recent post-season successes to hang hats on
- Feeling like there is nothing else you can do there

Experienced coaches realize these factors are not good indicators when changing jobs. They understand that every team has its own unique challenges. Yes, even those teams that win the title year after year. No one is immune from injuries, parents, a low talent pool, facility problems, losing a post-season game, or administrators that fail to be strong in times of crisis.

While we think about what might cause us to consider moving on, it may be prudent to explore some unfulfilling reasons we might use to justify a move.

- Less work
- Low Expectations
- No leadership or support
- Band-Aid job for a year
- Only other job available

All of us are competitors and have a driving passion for what we do. Taking a job that requires less of us, has soft expectations, and which encourages limited engagement to minimize problems is not a good situation. In addition, taking a job knowing you'll leave in a year, or because it's the only job available, is not fair to yourself or your employer. None of these scenarios will give you the challenging environment you are seeking. If you are a quality coach, being in a job with little or no expectations and no leadership is much worse than being in one with unrealistic expectations. Let's take a look at some of the reasons for changing jobs that have substance.

- Need for a bigger challenge

- The time is right for you and your family

- Your ability is in demand

- Leadership is strong at the other school and will help you grow

- You are familiar with the new school, administrators, and its program

While there may be other reasons, coaches continuously thrive on challenges. The ability to build, shape, bring people together, and more. When the challenge of your current team doesn't feed that hunger, it may be time to research other opportunities. Also, your family situation may prompt a move.

Coming off one (or several) successful seasons could make you very desirable for other programs, and frankly that desirability may never be that high again. The time may be just right. If the AD and administrators aren't giving you the direction and assessment necessary to be challenged, or there is no support for your facilities, it can be very frustrating. Even top coaches need guidance and financial support to field their team.

The program you're considering could be one you're familiar with through a colleague, former teammate, or former coach. You may even know the AD or other faculty at the school. If you've visited their campus, talked with them in depth and have a feeling that the move would be a good fit, it may be another good reason to do so.

It may be best to wait a while after the season is over to let the dust settle before making a decision regarding your job and situation. However, if you've considered it from every angle, moving on may be the best alternative. Timing is often crucial. The longer you stay at your current job and become comfortable, the more difficult it is to uproot the family.

Making a move can be scary and thrilling at the same time. Leaving a school where you've put your heart and soul into building a program is never easy. Just take your time to make the best decision possible for yourself and your family. Keep in mind that no job or administrator is perfect.

Thank You!

I want to thank you for reading our book; I hope it has affirmed some thoughts, experiences, and ideas you've entertained throughout your career. If you are beginning your new journey in the coaching profession I trust it has given you insight on other aspects of coaching that you may not have thought about.

My wish is that through all the clutter and distractions of coaching – such as paperwork, deadlines, travel plans, scheduling, and more – that you always make your players your number one priority. The guidance, leadership, and inspiration they need, and which you provide, can and will ultimately impact their lives. You have to ask yourself, is your impact positive or negative? Do you have their best interests at heart? Is this about winning a game, or much more?

When you think about the game you coach it's pretty constant, and hasn't changed much with respect to rules, and field or court sizes, in years. But players have. While they are bigger, stronger, faster and in some cases more skillful, they seem to be distracted today more than ever, and that can become a challenge. Or does it? You see distractions are not new. It will always be your ability to reach, relate, and guide your players through the maze back to refocusing on what is important. Through that process, you teach priorities in life such as family, career, responsibility, accountability, and commitment. All needed as they begin their lives.

Coaching is a noble profession, often misunderstood, overlooked, and underappreciated, but so worth it. It changed my life forever in a positive, rewarding way. I can assure you the difference you will make in your players' lives will be worth every minute.

I wish you the best in your career, and hope that all your dreams come true.

Keep inspiring!

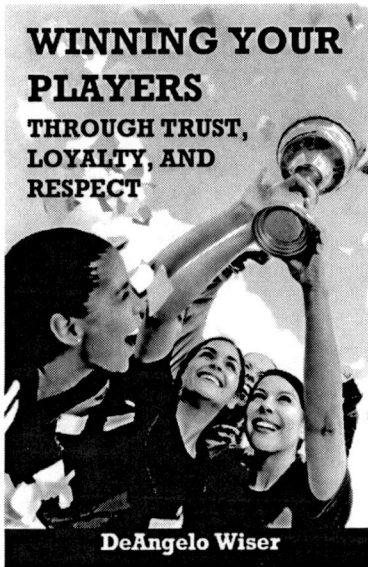

Winning Your Players through Trust, Loyalty, and Respect: A Soccer Coach's Guide

DeAngelo Wiser

In order to develop the best soccer players, who can achieve their very best in the game, a coach needs to instill three central qualities: Trust, Loyalty, and Respect. Without them, your words have no meaning and lack the power to inspire your players to reach new heights; with them, your team gains the ability and motivation to over-achieve.

Winning Your Players offers a clear pathway for coaches who want to develop and nurture talent to the best of their abilities, and gives insight into situations that require strong leadership at key moments with your team. In those moments we need every resource possible to clearly do what's best for our team. Winning Your Players is a must during those times.

Chapters include:

> Do You Trust Your Players?

> Eight Moments a Coach's Impact will never be Greater

> Can you handle the Truth?

> Over-coaching… can you hear it?

> …and many more

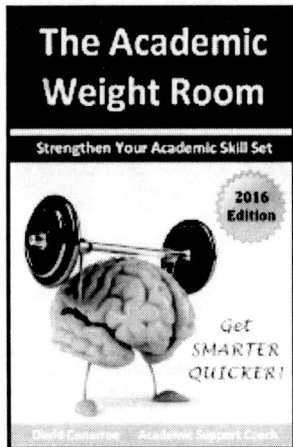

The Academic Weight Room: Strengthen Your Academic Skill Set

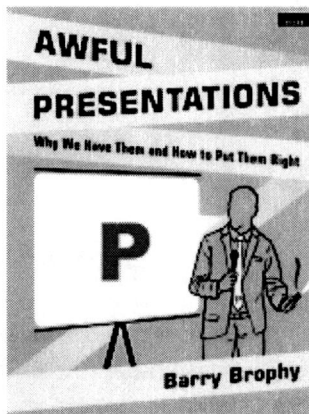

Awful Presentations: Why We Have Them and How to Put Them Right

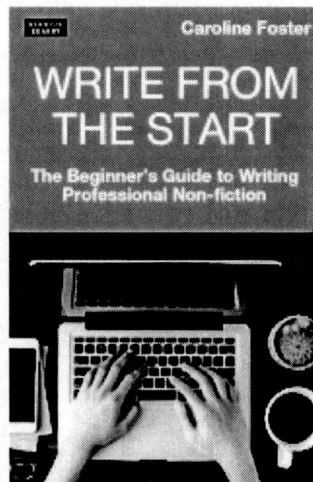

Write From The Start: The Beginner's Guide to Writing Professional Non-Fiction

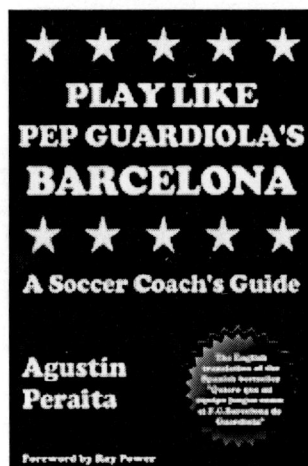

Play Like Pep Guardiola's Barcelona: A Soccer Coach's Guide

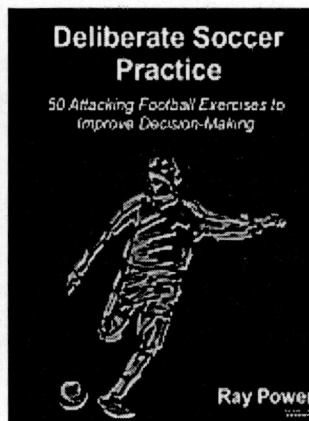

Deliberate Soccer Practice: 50 Attacking Exercises to Improve Decision-Making

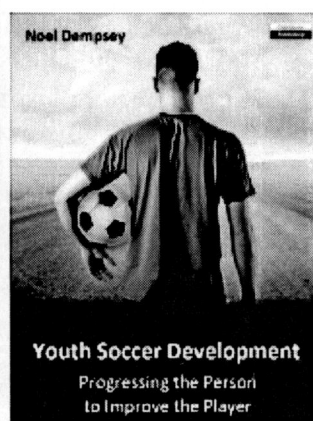

Youth Soccer Development: Progressing the Person to Improve the Player

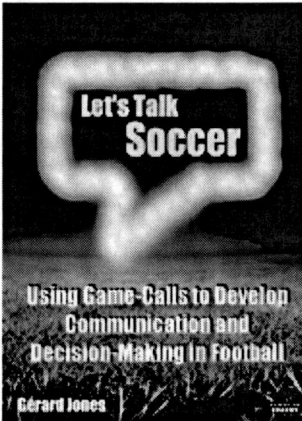

Let's Talk Soccer: Using Game-Calls to Develop Communication and Decision-Making in Football

The Modern Soccer Coach: Position-Specific Training

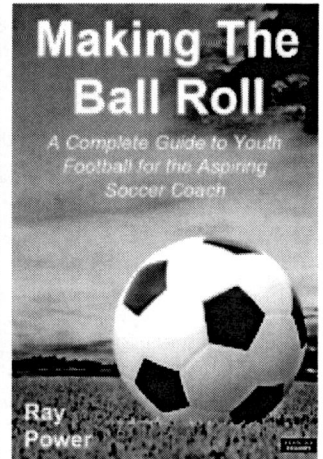

Making The Ball Roll: A Complete Guide to Youth Football for the Aspiring Soccer Coach

The Footballer's Journey: real-world advice on becoming and remaining a professional footballer

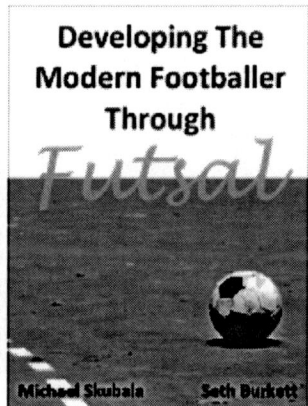

Developing the Modern Footballer through Futsal

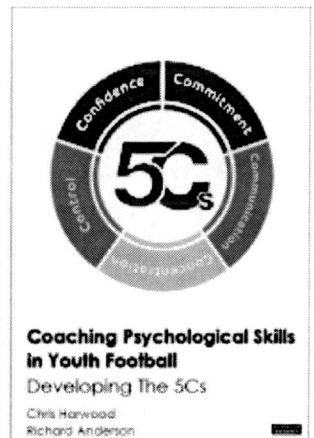

Coaching Psychological Skills in Youth Football: Developing The 5Cs

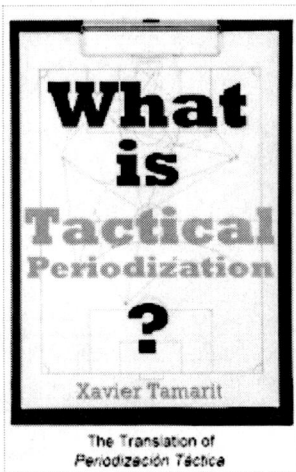

What is Tactical Periodization?

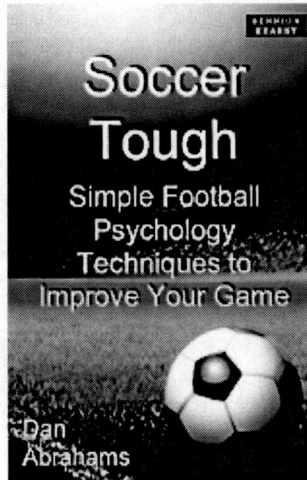

Soccer Tough: Simple Football Psychology Techniques to Improve Your Game

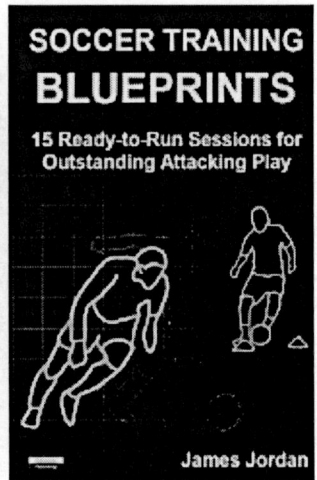

Soccer Training Blueprints: 15 Ready-to-Run Sessions for Outstanding Attacking Play

The Hidden Motor: The Psychology of Cycling

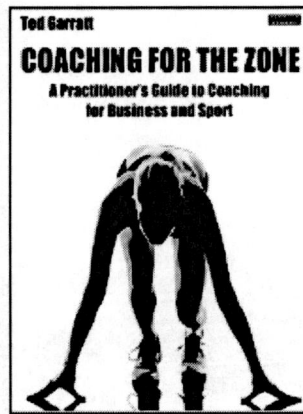

Coaching For The Zone: A Practitioner's Guide to Coaching for Business and Sport

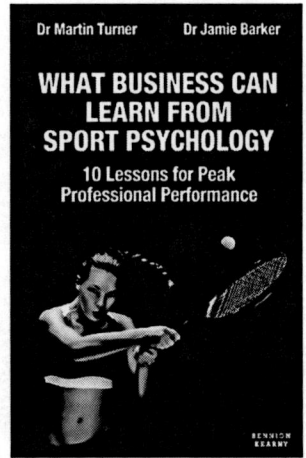

What Business Can Learn From Sport Psychology: Ten Lessons for Peak Professional Performance

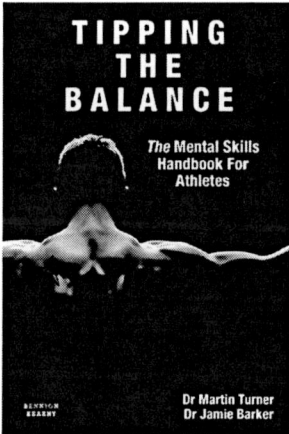

Tipping The Balance: The Mental Skills Handbook For Athletes [Sport Psychology Training Series]

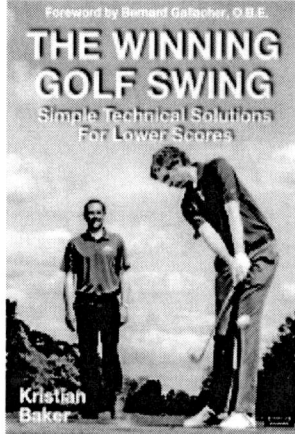

The Winning Golf Swing: Simple Technical Solutions for Lower Scores

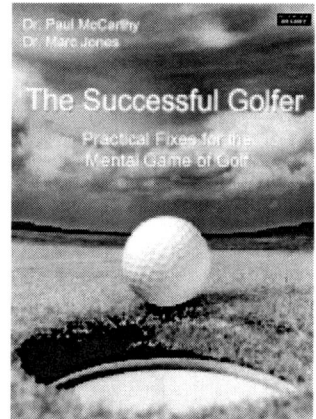

The Successful Golfer: Practical Fixes for the Mental Game of Golf

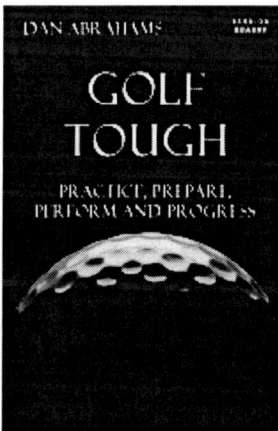

Golf Tough: Practice, Prepare, Perform and Progress

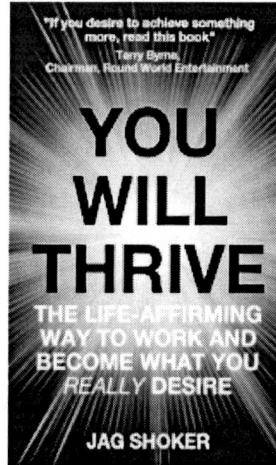

You Will Thrive: The Life-Affirming Way to Work and Become What You Really Desire

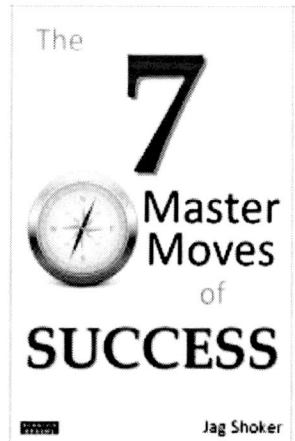

The 7 Master Moves of Success

See all our books at

www.BennionKearny.com

CPSIA information can be obtained
at www.ICGtesting.com
Printed in the USA
FFOW01n1747150318
45751700-46605FF